FACES

Christopher McHugh

Wayland

Discovering art

Animals
Faces
Food
People at Work
Town and Country
Water

Cover Senecio, *a face painted in 1922 by the Swiss artist Paul Klee. Kunstmuseum, Basle, Switzerland.*

Editor: Rosemary Ashley
Designer: David Armitage

First published in 1992 by
Wayland (Publishers) Limited
61 Western Road, Hove
East Sussex BN3 1JD
England

© Copyright 1992 Wayland (Publishers) Limited

British Library Cataloguing in Publication Data
McHugh, Christopher
   Faces. – (Discovering Art Series)
   I. Title.   II. Series
   704.942

   ISBN 0–7502–0510–5

Typeset by Type Study, Scarborough, England
Printed in Italy by G. Canale & C.S.p.A., Turin
Bound in Belgium by Casterman S.A.

Contents

1 Faces in art

A face is perhaps the first thing that we recognize with our eyes. Young babies soon begin to respond to the sight of their mother's face, and later on to those of other people.

We all learn to understand what the expressions on people's faces mean; angry or sad, happy or unsure. We use our faces to show much more than we can say in words. We look at people's faces to see if they are telling the truth, or making a joke, or lying. Through thousands of years, actors have used their faces, or masks which represent faces, to help show the meaning of the play or dance which they are performing.

When you first made a picture of a face it was probably just a circle, perhaps with two dots for eyes and two lines for the nose and mouth. Try now and see if you can make a really simple drawing that is still a recognizable face. Try making a face using lots of different shapes. Look at the simple shapes Paul Klee has used to make the face in his picture, *Senecio*, shown on the cover of this book.

There are faces in just about every kind of art, made with all sorts of materials. Picture **1** shows a huge stone carving of a face made by the Olmec people, who lived 2,000 years ago in the country that is now Mexico. The carving was made by chipping away little bits of an enormous block of stone, to finally leave the shape of the head standing free.

In the following pages you will see and read about many kinds of art, showing faces from different times and from countries all over the world.

1 (opposite) *This gigantic stone figure was carved by the Olmec people, who belonged to a very early civilization living in Mexico between two and three thousand years ago. It is at La Venta in Mexico.*

2 Ancient faces

We can often see faces in art from ancient civilizations such as that of Egypt, in books, museums and films. During the thousands of years of the Ancient Egyptian civilization, many pictures and sculptures were made showing faces. But we see fewer faces made by the people who lived in Mesopotamia, the area which we now call the Middle East. Their civilizations were as old as Egypt, but very little of their art remains because they did not have many long-lasting building materials available, such as stone.

Picture **2** is a rare example of a Sumerian painting. The people of Sumer were among the earliest of those who lived in Mesopotamia. The painting dates from about 2600 BC and is rather like a cartoon in the way it shows people. See how the artist has picked out the important features to draw most clearly – noses, eyes, the shape of heads, ears, eyebrows . . .

2 A Sumerian picture showing a musician playing a lyre to celebrate a victory in battle. The man on the left is an army officer and the woman behind is a singer. British Museum, London.

3 *The head and shoulders of a statue of the Egyptian Princess Nofret. The statue is one of a pair – the other is of her husband Prince Rahotep. Egyptian Museum, Cairo.*

4 (below) *The gold mask of Tutankhamun, the Egyptian boy king who ruled Egypt in the thirteenth century* BC. *He was only eighteen when he died and was buried in Thebes in a coffin with this mask at its head. Egyptian Museum, Cairo.*

These two Egyptian heads are both sculptures. Picture **3** shows a stone sculpture of a princess called Nofret. It has been painted to pick out certain features more clearly, especially the princess' clothes and the make-up which she often used. Take a look at picture **31** on page 27. Both these pictures show a woman with make-up on. What are the differences between the two pictures?

The head of King Tutankhamun, picture **4**, is made from gold and is part of the rich coffin made for his preserved body, called a mummy. The mummy was found, with this marvellous mask and many other treasures, in a tomb inside a pyramid in Egypt.

5 *A bronze head of the Greek god Apollo. It was found in Cyprus and is now in the British Museum, London.*

6 (below) *A marble sculpture of the head of the Roman Emperor Hadrian, who ruled from AD 117–138. British Museum, London.*

Picture **5** is a sculpture from the period known as Classical Greece (around 500–300 BC). It shows the head of the god Apollo. The sculpture is made from a metal called bronze, through a process called casting. To cast an object a mould has first to be made. If you think of pressing something into clay or plasticine and then carefully removing it, that will give you an idea of how a mould can be made. Then a liquid substance is poured into the mould and allowed to set. In the case of bronze, it has to be heated until it melts, setting hard again as it cools. Pictures **11** and **15** on pages 12 and 15 also show bronze castings.

The Romans learned a great deal from the Greeks, especially about art. Picture **6** is a sculpture of the Roman Emperor Hadrian. It is much more a portrait of the actual person than the Greek god Apollo (picture **5**) or Tutankhamun's golden mask (picture **4**).

Picture **7** is a mosaic, which is a picture made by gluing small pieces of coloured stone onto a floor or wall. This mosaic comes from Cirencester in England and it shows how the Romans took their art to all parts of their enormous empire. Look how the face is shown, using simple, heavily outlined shapes, filled in with the little coloured pieces.

7 Part of a mosaic on the floor of a Roman villa in Corinum, present-day Cirencester, England. The mosaic shows the four seasons – this is of Autumn.

3 Faces in art around the world

Here are three pictures of faces made by the original peoples of North and South America (see also picture **1**). Picture **8** is a painting made by the Aztecs. Like the Olmecs, who made the stone sculpture in picture **1**, the Aztecs also lived in the area now called Mexico, but many centuries later. The painting shows the sun god (top left) and the god of darkness (below) and is actually a kind of writing in pictures. The strong outlines and clear colours make it look like a modern cartoon. If you compare this

8 *A page from an Aztec sacred book called a codex. The Aztecs lived in Mexico in the fifteenth century. Their sacred books contained 'picture writing' which could be understood by different tribes who spoke different languages. University Library, Bologna, Italy.*

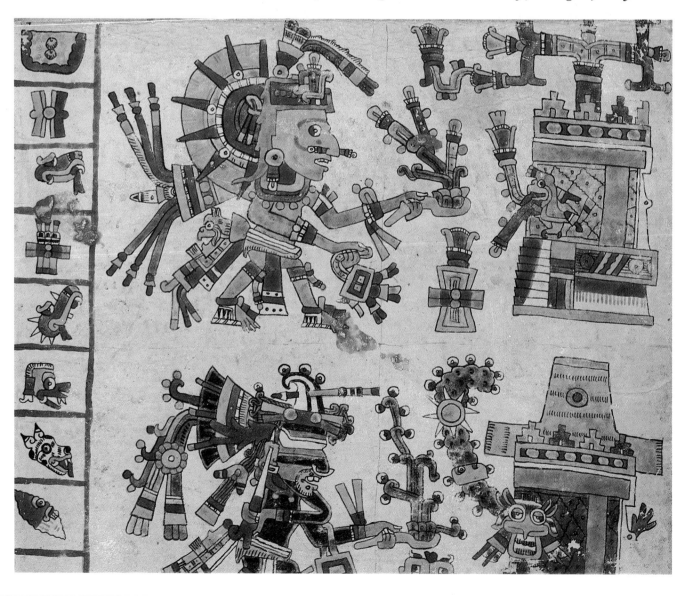

9 *The painted wooden mask of a Tsimshian girl. It has human hair, and wooden hair decorations in the shape of birds with hinged wings. Portland Art Museum, Oregon, USA.*

10 (below) *The mask of a dancer used by the Kwakiutl tribespeople living in Canada. Field Museum of National History, Chicago, USA.*

picture with picture **2** (page 6), you can see that although the clothes the gods are wearing are more important, the whole picture also makes a flat pattern.

Faces often appear in the art of the tribespeople living on the north-west coast of North America. Picture **9** is a mask of a girl from the Tsimshian tribe. It is quite life-like and uses real human hair to make it look even more real. Picture **10**, a carved wooden mask, is much less like a real person's face. It has a hooked bird beak for a nose, hands for cheeks, simple eyes, mouth and ears, and a plaited string for hair and beard. It was made by the Kwakiutl tribe and would have been used as part of the costume in special tribal dances.

The huge continent of Africa, with its many different peoples, has a very ancient history. The earliest human beings are thought to have lived in Africa. The pictures here show two of the many different ways of making faces in art that can be found in Africa.

Picture **11** (like picture **5** on page 8) is another bronze casting, made in West Africa over six hundred years ago. It is very like a real person's face. Picture **12** is very different from picture **11**. It is a wooden carving covered with a sheet of metal, which has had a pattern of dents beaten into it. It was made by the BaKota people of Gabon, in West Africa. Can you see how the face is made from very unrealistic shapes; notice the cross in which the nose and eyes appear.

11 (above) *A bronze head made by a West African sculptor about five hundred years ago. British Museum, London.*

12 *A head made from wood covered with beaten brass, made by the BaKotu people in West Africa. Entwistle Gallery, London.*

13 *A carved wooden mask made by a Maori craftsman in New Zealand. Aukland Institute and Museum, New Zealand.*

The carved wooden Maori mask from New Zealand, picture **13**, is covered with a pattern of tattoos, in circles, coils and parallel lines. Can you see how the patterns are a little like the unrealistic shapes of the face in picture **12**? The shapes and patterns in pictures like **12** and **13** had a great influence on modern artists, for instance Picasso, Jawlensky and Klee (see pictures **29** and **30** on pages 26 and 27 and the cover picture).

This book shows several ways in which people have made sculptures of faces. The process of casting was described on page 8, and there are examples of carved wood and stone – for instance pictures **1** and **13** (pages 5 and 13). Picture **14**, like picture **12** on page 12, is an example of beaten metal work. This time the metal used is silver. The picture shows the face of a god on part of a cauldron from Northern Europe. It was made by the Celts about the year AD 1000. See how the artist has used strong, clear lines for this face, for instance in the eyebrows and sides of the moustache.

14 *The face of a Celtic god, on the side of a cauldron made from beaten silver. National Museum, Copenhagen, Denmark.*

15 *The bronze head of a Buddha made in the seventeenth century in Thailand.*

16 (below) *An ancient stone carving of a man's head, from China.*

Picture **15** is a bronze cast statue from Thailand. It shows the head of the eastern religious teacher known as the Buddha. Picture **16** shows a Chinese head that has been carved from stone. Can you see that both these sculptures express calmness and peacefulness? Gently curving shapes and lines have been used to create this calm and peaceful feeling. But look how much clearer and sharper the lines are that the Thai artist has used, for instance on the eyebrows, down the nose, around the lips and for the eyelids. The Chinese face is very much rounder, fuller and more solid.

4 Greek and Roman influences

Picture **17** shows a painting on a wooden panel. It is a portrait made to be placed on a coffin – like the golden head of Tutankhamun, picture **4**, page 7. The face was painted in Egypt about 2,000 years ago, during the time when Egypt was part of the Roman Empire. This style of painting is called Graeco-Roman because the style was invented by the Greeks but later used by artists all over the Roman Empire.

Picture **18** is a mosaic made by a Christian artist living in the Byzantine Empire (present-day Greece and Turkey) at the end of the twelfth century. The mosaic is a little like picture **17** above. It shows the same long nose and heavy eyelids but this image of Jesus Christ is not at all like an image of a real person.

17 (above) A Man with a Wreath – *a portrait painted on a wooden panel, made in Egypt about the year AD 1. The National Gallery, London.*

18 *A mosaic of Jesus Christ dating from the twelfth century. It is in a church in present-day Greece.*

19 Jeanne Hebuterne *a portrait painted by the twentieth-century Italian artist Amedeo Modigliani. Christies, London.*

Picture **19** is by the twentieth century artist Amedeo Modigliani. Can you see how he has used some ideas about painting faces from the art shown in pictures **17** and **18**? Look at the long stretched shape of the face and the clear, curving outlines. This is just one example of the influence of Classical Greece and Rome on art of later times.

5 The Renaissance

20 Mona Lisa *by Leonardo da Vinci – the world's most famous portrait. The Louvre, Paris.*

The period known as the Renaissance began in Italy in about the fourteenth century. It was a time when earlier Greek and Roman ideas were rediscovered and became popular. Two of the greatest artists of this time and two of the best-known of any time, are the Italians Leonardo da Vinci and Michelangelo. Both men were fascinated by people and by faces.

Picture **20** shows one of the most famous paintings of a face in the world. It is *Mona Lisa* by Leonardo. It is a portrait of a mysterious woman in front of a background of countryside. People often ask why is the picture so famous, and why is *Mona Lisa* just beginning to smile? Many people have tried to answer these two questions, but no one can agree who is right.

Michelangelo was a very famous sculptor as well as a great painter. One of his best-known works is the huge painting he made to cover the ceiling of the Sistine Chapel in the Vatican in Rome. Picture **21** is a small section of this painting, showing the Bible story of God separating the land from the seas as He creates the world. God is shown as an old man, with fluffy beard and hair and wrinkly skin, a rather different image than that of Jesus Christ in picture **18** on page 16. Michelangelo's painting is a fresco, which means it is painted straight on to a plaster wall (or ceiling) and becomes part of the surface of the wall itself.

21 *A detail from the painting of the creation of the world by Michelangelo, on the ceiling of the Sistine Chapel in the Vatican in Rome.*

The ideas of the Renaissance started in Italy and gradually spread throughout Europe. They were soon taken up in the Netherlands, in the region that is now Belgium. Picture **22** is by one of the earliest of the great painters of the Netherlands, Rogier van der Weyden. Although most of the pictures painted at this time were still of subjects concerned with the Christian religion, van der Weyden was beginning, like other artists, to paint portraits of real people. Picture **22** shows a woman of the period as she actually looked. See how her eyes sparkle.

22 Portrait of a Woman *by Rogier van der Weyden. Staatlilche Gemalde-Gallerie, Berlin, Germany.*

23 *A self-portrait by Rembrandt van Rijn, one of many that he made to mark the stages of his life. Kenwood House, London.*

Rembrandt's portrait of himself (picture **23**) is also from the Netherlands, but it is from Holland which is further north, and painted about two hundred years later. It was made not to sell but as a record of the artist's own appearance. Like picture **22**, it is also an oil painting, but Rembrandt has used the paint in a different way to van der Weyden. Can you see how differently? Look at how the two artists have shown the edges of things, and how they have shown light and shadow. Rembrandt painted many self-portraits and they form a special set of paintings, sometimes thought to be his greatest work, recording how he changed through the years of his long life.

6 Weird faces

Until the invention of photography in the mid-nineteenth century, many forms of art needed to show people's faces as they actually looked. But this has not been the only reason why artists have liked to show faces. Many have used faces in their art to express their feelings about people or the world in which they live.

The three paintings on these pages deliberately show strange faces. Hieronymus Bosch was an artist with strong religious beliefs. He lived at the time of the Reformation, when great changes were taking place in the Christian Church. In his painting (picture **24**) showing Jesus Christ before his crucifixion, he shows the cruelty and wickedness which causes such suffering.

Bosch has painted the people's clothes and their tools to show this cruelty, but even more importantly, he has shown the evil character and behaviour of those who tortured Christ in the ugliness and cruelty of their faces.

Giuseppe Arcimboldi's strange picture of a face made out of fruit and vegetables (picture **25**) is typical of many of his paintings. It is a way of showing a fantastic view of familiar things. The painting is meant to surprise and amuse those who look at it.

24 Christ crowned with thorns *by Hieronymus Bosch. The National Gallery, London.*

25 Whimsical Portrait *A strange picture of fruit, nuts and vegetables that form a face, by Giuseppe Arcimboldi. Nostell Priory, Yorkshire, England.*

26 Old Woman *by Francisco de Goya. He painted these witch-like figures late in his life, when he often showed frightening images, both real and imagined. Musée de Beaux Arts, Lille, France.*

Francisco de Goya was a Spanish artist who lived through a very difficult period in his country's history, when Spain was fighting the armies of the French Emperor Napoleon. During this time Goya saw many terrible things. In his later life he also suffered an illness which caused him to become deaf. He began to paint terrifying pictures of monsters, horrible-looking people and gruesome acts of war. Often he used faces to show the awfulness of his subjects, as in picture **26**. How has Goya made these old women look so horrible?

7 Modern faces

27 Head of a young girl, *a portrait made in pastels by Mary Cassatt. Musée de Petit Palais, Paris.*

The modern period of art is usually said to have begun in the second half of the nineteenth century. Mary Cassatt was an American artist who lived and worked in France at that time, with the group of artists who became known as the Impressionists. In picture **27** we see a painting she made of a small child. She used a special kind of chalk, called pastel, to make this picture. Much of the picture is left only partly finished, but the face has had a lot more work done on it. Can you see where Cassatt has left areas of the paper blank, and where she has made rapid marks almost like scribbling?

Vincent Van Gogh is now a very famous artist, although during his lifetime hardly anybody had heard of him. Picture **28** is a self-portrait made after he had injured himself by deliberately cutting off a piece of his ear. Van Gogh was Dutch but he spent the last years of his life as a painter in France. There he saw the work of the Impressionists and he used many of their ideas in his art. Can you see the brushmarks in his painting? They are left clearly showing in parts of the picture. These brushmarks, and the bright colours Van Gogh has used, give the picture a sort of energy or sense of movement.

28 *A self-portrait painted by Vincent Van Gogh after he had cut off part of his ear while feeling very upset. Courtauld Galleries, London.*

Pablo Picasso was a Spanish artist who, like Van Gogh, spent much time in France. Picture **29** shows the head of a woman who, the title tells us, is weeping. Can you see the handkerchief and the tears? Picasso has used heavy dark lines to draw the shapes which make up the woman's face. Would you say this picture is anything like picture **12**, on page 12, and if so, why? In this book, can you find any other pictures from earlier times which are a little like Picasso's painting?

29 Weeping Woman *by Pablo Picasso. Private collection.* © *DACS 1992.*

The picture on the cover of this book, called *Senecio*, is by a Swiss artist, Paul Klee. Picture **30** is by a Russian artist, Alexej von Jawlensky. Both these artists worked for a time in Germany, with other artists who called themselves The Blue Rider Group, in the early years of the twentieth century. Can you see any likenesses in their two pictures? Colours and shapes are very important in each.

In picture **30**, Jawlensky uses colours and shapes to produce a mood or feeling rather than to describe a real face. Klee's picture, on the cover, is also of an imaginary face, but with more definite edges. Like Picasso, in picture **29**, Klee shows the side view of the nose in his painting and the front view of both eyes. Can you see how each artist has done this? Now take another look at picture **2** (page 6). Can you see how the artist here has also shown a front view of the eye and a side view of the nose on each person's face?

Picture **31** is by the American artist Andy Warhol. It is a screen print showing a famous film star called Marilyn Monroe. The features of her face are drawn with the black layer and then simple, flat shapes of colour are put on to certain areas – pink skin, yellow hair, red lips, blue eyelids. The black layer of the print is taken from a photograph. The coloured areas show the make-up that Marilyn was well-known for – bright lipstick, bleached hair, heavy eye-shadow. Warhol's pictures often point out the difference between the real thing, and pictures of the real thing which we see so often in our modern world in magazines, television and films.

30 Symphony in Rose *by Alexej von Jawlensky, Frankfurt, Germany.*

31 Marilyn, *Andy Warhol's screen print of Marilyn Monroe, made in 1967.* ©*ARS.*

Who are the artists and where are their works?

Giuseppe Arcimboldi (1527–93) Italian
An artist who became very famous during his lifetime for paintings of faces made up of objects such as vegetables, flowers and fruit. His work can be seen in some of the larger collections of paintings in European cities. Picture **25**, page 22.

Hieronymus Bosch (c.1450–1516) Dutch
A painter of strange and fantastic pictures, many of them expressing religious ideas. Little is known about his early life but he lived and worked in the Netherlands, in the town of 's Hertogenbosch, from which his name is taken. Bosch's work can be seen in important collections all over the world, including the Louvre in Paris, the National Gallery, London and the Metropolitan Museum, New York. Picture **24**, page 22.

Mary Cassatt (1845–1926) American
An Impressionist painter whose favourite subjects were women and children. She was greatly influenced by Japanese prints. Her work can be seen in many important American collections such as in Baltimore, Philadelphia and New York, and also in major European galleries. Picture **27**, page 24.

Vincent Van Gogh (1853–90) Dutch
He was born in the Netherlands but painted many of his best-known pictures in France. He was influenced by the work of Dutch painters of the past, by the clear, bright colours of Japanese prints, and most importantly, by the Impressionist painters. Like the Impressionists, Van Gogh painted pictures of people and things around him. His work can be seen in important collections all over the world, and especially in the Musée d'Orsay in Paris and Van Gogh Museum in Amsterdam; also in the National, Tate and Courtauld Galleries in London. Picture **28**, page 25.

Francisco de Goya (1746–1828) Spanish
He became a successful court painter, painting many portraits of the royal family and other important people, but he often showed unfavourable sides of their characters. In 1808 the French invaded Spain and Goya worked on a series of famous prints called *The Disasters of War*, which showed the cruelty and horror of war. His work can be seen in major collections all over the world, especially in the Prado in Madrid, at the National and Courtauld Galleries in London, and the National Gallery and Phillips Collection in Washington. Picture **26**, page 23.

Alexej von Jawlensky (1864–1941) Russian
A painter who, after spending some time in the Russian army, studied and worked in Germany from about 1896. In his later life he formed a group called the Blue Four, with three other well-known painters, including Paul Klee. His work can be seen in certain major collections, especially in Pasadena, USA and Wiesbaden, Germany. Picture **30**, page 27.

Paul Klee (1879–1940) Swiss/German
A printer and painter who studied and worked in Switzerland and Germany. His travels in North Africa influenced his feeling for colour. Klee was connected to the 'Blue Rider' and 'Blue Four' groups of painters in Germany, along with Alexej von Jawlensky. His work can be seen in collections of modern art throughout the world and especially at the Klee Foundation, Berne, Switzerland. Cover picture.

Leonardo da Vinci (1452–1519) Italian
A brilliant artist, scientist and inventor who lived during the Renaissance. He is one of the most famous of all European artists. The *Mona Lisa* is probably Leonardo's most famous work. Few of his paintings and inventions were completed, but the huge quantity of notes and drawings which he left behind are among the greatest works of the Renaissance. Major works can be seen in Italy, and in Paris, Washington, and the National Gallery in London. The best collection of Leonardo's drawings is in the Royal Library at Windsor Castle, near London. Picture **20**, page 18.

Michelangelo Buonarroti (1475–1564) Italian
Along with Leonardo and Raphael, he is considered to be the greatest artist of the Renaissance. Like Leonardo, Michelangelo had many talents – he is probably most famous as a sculptor, although the painting on the ceiling of the Sistine Chapel is also a world-famous work. He was also well-known as a poet. Michelangelo's works can be seen especially in Italy, and in the National Gallery, Royal Academy and British Museum in London. Picture **21**, page 19.

Amedeo Modigliani (1884–1920) Italian
A sculptor and painter who worked mainly in Paris. Modigliani was a brilliant draughtsman. He is best known for his pictures of people whose heads and features he usually elongated (made longer). His works can be seen in major collections around the world, and in the Tate Gallery, the Victoria and Albert Museum and the Courtauld Gallery, London. Picture **19**, page 17.

Pablo Picasso (1881–1973) Spanish
He was born in Malaga, Spain, but after a visit to Paris in 1900, he lived permanently in France. He was one of the leading experimenters in art. With Georges Braque, he invented the style of art called Cubism. Picasso was perhaps the greatest artist of the twentieth century and turned out a huge amount of work. His work can be seen in major galleries all over the world. Picture **29**, page 26.

Rembrandt van Rijn (1606–69) Dutch
One of the greatest of all Dutch painters. Early in his career he was a successful painter of large pictures of religious and classical stories. Later he earned his living as a portrait painter. Throughout his career he painted portraits, of himself which reflected his advancing years and changing mood. Many believe them to be his finest work. His work can be seen in galleries all over the world, especially in Holland, and at the National Gallery, Kenwood House, Wallace Collection (all in London), also in Cambridge, Edinburgh, Glasgow, Liverpool, and Dublin in Eire. There is a huge collection of his drawings and etchings in his house in Amsterdam. Picture **23**, page 21.

Andy Warhol (1930–1987) American
An American artist who invented a kind of art which came to be known as 'Pop Art' because it used images and objects that people see and use every day. Warhol especially made use of familiar products on sale in their millions, such as tinned soup and newspaper photographs, often making bright coloured screen prints of them. His work can be seen in major collections of modern art all over the world. Picture **31**, page 27.

Rogier van der Weyden (c.1399–1464) Flemish
He is one the most important Flemish painters of the fifteenth century. Van der Weyden was very successful and became City Painter in Brussels. His paintings express feelings much more than most other Flemish painters of the same period. His work can be seen in major collections around the world and in the National Gallery, London. Picture **22**, page 20.

Glossary

Bronze A type of metal, made from copper and tin and used for making tools and sculpture.

Brushmarks The marks left by a brush in a painting.

Byzantine Empire The Roman Empire in the East, founded by Emperor Constantine I, who moved from Rome to Constantinople (now Istanbul) in the fourth century AD.

Cartoon An amusing drawing making fun of something or someone.

Casting Producing a shape by pouring or pressing liquid wax, plastic, bronze or other metal into a mould.

Cauldron A large, heavy pot, used for boiling liquids.

Celts A people who settled all over western Europe, in pre-Roman times.

Civilization A stage in the development of the way people live together in groups.

Christian Someone who practises the religion based on the teachings of Jesus Christ.

Classical Relating to the Ancient Greeks and Romans.

Crucifixion The death of Jesus Christ on the cross.

Draughtsman Someone skilled in drawing.

Egyptian mummy An embalmed or preserved body that was prepared for burial in Ancient Egypt.

Fresco A way of painting straight on to newly-plastered walls or ceilings.

Graeco-Roman The period from around 100 BC to AD 100, when art was influenced by Greek and Roman styles.

Impressionists A group of artists painting at the end of the nineteenth century in France.

Mosaic A picture or pattern made by gluing pieces of stone or glass into a floor or wall.

Mould A shape into which a melted liquid substance is poured. The substance takes on the shape of the mould as it hardens.

Oil painting A painting either on stretched canvas or wood, where the artist uses a type of paint in which the colour is held together with linseed or poppy seed oil.

Pastels Coloured, chalky crayons.

Portrait A picture of a person intended to be a record of what that person looks like.

Pyramid A triangular structure built by the Ancient Egyptians for the Tombs of their Kings.

Reformation The religious movement of the sixteenth century which resulted in the establishment of Protestant Churches.

Renaissance A time of rediscovery in Europe of ideas from Ancient Greece and Rome.

Roman Empire The territories ruled by Ancient Rome. The head of the Empire was called the emperor.

Screen print A print made with cloth, where the ink is pressed through the weave.

Sculpture The art of carving, casting or modelling statues and designs.

Self-portrait A picture painted by the artist of him or herself.

Tattoos Designs made on the skin by pricking and staining it.

Unrealistic Not having a believeable appearance.

Villa In Ancient Rome, a large country house.

Books to read

The Book of Art – A Way of Seeing (Ernest Benn, 1979).

Every Picture Tells a Story by Rolf Harris (Phaidon, 1989).

Faces – Looking at Art by Giles Waterfield (Wayland, 1983).

Families – through the eyes of artists by Wendy and Jack Richardson (Macmillan, 1990).

Great Painters by Piero Ventura (Kingfisher, 1989).

Just Look . . . A Book about Paintings by Robert Cumming (Viking Kestrel, 1986).

Painting and Sculpture by Jillian Powell (Wayland, 1989).

Penguin Dictionary of Art and Artists by Peter and Linda Murray (Penguin, 1989).

20th Century Art by Jillian Powell (Wayland, 1989).

Picture acknowledgements

The publishers have attempted to contact all copyright holders of the illustrations in this title, and apologise if there have been any oversights.

The photographs in this book were supplied by: The Ancient Art and Architecture Collection © Ronald Sheridan 7 (lower); Bridgeman Art Library cover, 17, 18, 19, 20, 22 (both), 24, 27 (both). Courtauld Institute/Bridgeman 25; Giraudon/Bridgeman 23; Kenwood House/Bridgeman 21; Michael Holford © 6, 8 (top), 9, 12 (top), 16 (lower), 26. National Gallery/C. McHugh 16 (top); Werner Forman Archive 5, 7 (top), 8 (lower), 10, 11 (both), 12 (lower), 13, 14, 15 (both).

Photographs of the following paintings appear by kind permission of the copyright holders: *Weeping Woman* by Pablo Picasso DACS 1992; and *Marilyn* by Andy Warhol. © 1992 The Andy Warhol Foundation for the Visual Arts/ARS, New York.

Index

Jute
Handlooms of India

Jute
Handlooms of India

MAPIN PUBLISHING PVT. LTD.

First Published by
Mapin Publishing Pvt. Ltd. 31, Somnath Road,
Usmanpura, Ahmedabad 380013 India
email: mapinpub@vsnl.com
on behalf of Ministry of Textiles,
Government of India

USA:
Grantha Corporation
80 Cliffedgeway, Middletown, NJ 07701

Distributed in North America by
Antique Collectors' Club
Market Street Industrial Park
Wappingers' Falls, NY 12590
Tel: 800-252-5231
Fax: 914-297-0068
website: www.antiquecc.com

Distributed in United Kingdom & Europe by
Antique Collectors' Club
5 Church Street, Woodbridge
Suffolk IP12 IDS, UK
Tel: 1394 385 501
Fax: 1394 384 434
email: accvs@aol.com

This edition as published © Mapin Publishing
Text & Photographs © Crafts Museum, New Delhi
except pages 10, 11, 14, 17, 18, 19, 23, 24, 25
courtesy Dr. K. Jayachardan, Director, Indian Jute
Industries Research Association, Calcutta and
pages 26, 27, 28 photographs by Samir Pathak,
courtesy NIFT Resource Centre, New Delhi

ISBN: 81-85822-65-4
ISBN: 1-890206-18-0
LC: 99-74702

Text by L V Saptarishi
Edited by Mallika Sarabhai
Designed by Jatin Banker / Mapin Design Studio
Printed by Ajanta Offset, New Delhi, India
Case cover fabric produced by Shri Puja Handloom
& Handicraft & Garments co-operative, New Delhi

CONTENTS

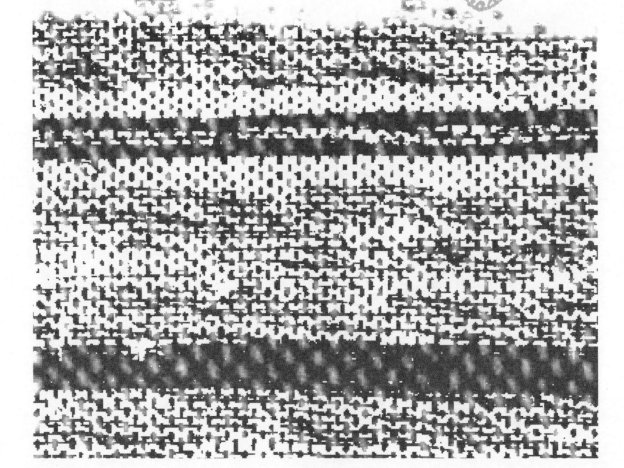

INTRODUCTION

From Rags to Riches

India has been home to almost all of the world's most important natural fibres. Besides cotton, wool and silk, India produced jute, hemp, rhea and several other fibres that even a hundred years ago were considered important items of trade. Cotton, wool, silk and jute are today grown or produced in different parts of the country, and their processing has given birth to one of the world's most important textile industries, whose products still reach far across the globe.

The availability of these raw materials has enabled the creation of a vast variety of products, woven domestically on handlooms or on industrial powerlooms and encompassing a seemingly endless array of uses, designs and decorations.

But amongst these four fibres jute has, until now, remained the poor relation. While silk, cotton and wool adorned ceremonies, furnishings or fashion parades, jute seemed condemned eternally to its use as humble sacking, for packaging or temporary coverings on construction sites.

Now that is set to change. Jute, at last, has a new future.

Jute–the History

While nobody can pinpoint the first human use of jute it was certainly known, and used from the times of India's great epics, the *Mahabharata* and the *Ramayana*. In the Sabha Parva section of the Mahabharata, the Kaurava prince Duryodhana tells his father of the gifts received by his cousin Yudhishthira at a ceremony that he has just attended. Amongst the many things listed are gems, jewels, grasses, clothes made of grasses and cloth woven from jute.

The *Ramayana* tells of how Hanuman, the monkey god, on his mission to rescue Sita from the King of Lanka, Ravana, was captured. On the orders of Ravana his long tail was set alight. The material used to bind and burn his tale was jute.

The author H.D.Goyal in his book *Indian Jute Industry: Problems and Prospects* also mentions the 16th century Bengali book *Kavikankan Chandi* by Mukundaram Chakravarty where there are references to jute bags.

Another mention of the use of jute during this period is in the *Ain-i-Akbari*. In the English translation of this book by Jarret, the author identifies *tat* as jute cloth from the Bengal region.

Till the middle of the 19th century, jute was being manufactured in India by peasants in the handloom sector and used as sacking and for a variety of cordage purposes. No organized production existed and its farming and manufacturing centred on Bengal. The first commercial mention of jute, according to the 1886 Colonial and Indian Exhibition catalogue, London, is in the customs report for exports from India in the year 1828. In that year, Rs 620 worth of raw jute was exported to Europe. There is no mention of jute manufactured goods being exported which indicates that all the sacks and rope made were indigenously used.

The outbreak of the Crimean War in 1854 gave a great fillip to India's jute exports. The mills of Dundee had depended on Russian hemp being imported into Scotland for their packaging needs but the war disrupted supplies for several years. Indian jute replaced the hemp. Jute was not completely unknown in Europe at that time. The Napoleonic wars had often before disrupted hemp supplies and the Dundee mills had started looking for a replacement for it. But before jute could completely replace hemp a technological problem had to be solved.

According to Omkar Goswami in *Industry, Trade and Peasant Society: The Jute Economy of Eastern India 1900-1947*, the main technological problem was of strengthening the coarse and brittle jute fabric so that it could be used for high speed spinning and weaving. "In 1832 the firm of Balfour and Melville overcame the problem by sprinkling raw jute with a suspension of whale oil and water. The new process was put to the test in 1838, when the Dundee mills were awarded a large Dutch order for manufacturing Javanese sugar bags. The jute bags were accepted, and burlap came to stay."

With the rapid increase in the exports of raw jute British entrepreneurs saw a good opportunity for investment. World trade was increasing and the demand for gunny bags would increase with it. Introducing powerlooms, with their very basic technology, would be easy and Indian labour would be much cheaper than that in Dundee. As jute manufacture was situated around Calcutta, a good port was also available for easy exports. In 1854, the Ishara Yarn Mills was the first to be established, in Serampore. Three years later the Baranagore Jute Mills was established and 20 others followed in the next few years. The value of foreign trade in jute, £ 62 in 1828, rose to £ 6,205,238 by 1885. However the trade in raw jute remained four times higher than the exports of jute bags. According to the Colonial and Indian Exhibition catalogue, "There were exported 41,523,607 power-loom made gunny bags; but, according to the Calcutta brokers, there were sold in Calcutta over and above 77,519,164 gunny bags. About one half of these are shown in the Government reports of coasting and railway-borne trade to have been sent from Bengal to other provinces to be used in the home and foreign grain trade."

In the 1884-85 *Review of the Trade of India*, Mr. J.E.Connor estimated that trade of jute had crossed the Rs. 3 crore mark.

By the end of the century, jute manufacture was almost entirely for exports. Nearly all the mills were owned by entrepreneurs from Scotland and many even had their management boards there. By 1900 exports had gone up to Rs. 7 crores. However this rapid growth soon levelled off with increasing competition from Scotland, Germany and the US, where the governments took on protectionist policies to encourage their own industry. The First World War gave another spurt to the growth of Indian jute as jute was used for sand bags, tarpaulins, tents, canvas cloth and wagon covers. But this spurt tapered off at the end of the War leading to over-production and a voluntary curtailment of production over the next two decades.

The next fifty years saw a gradual decline in the industry a near stagnation, being reached by the early '80s. The number of mills went down to 22 from the 112 that were up and running at Independence.

For over a hundred years, jute had been used for the production of sacking and sacks. As other fibres became more and more varied, almost all the production of jute remained confined to these forms. A mindset was established that jute had no other possibilities. As a result no new technology was applied, no experiments carried out. Only in the last decade of the twentieth century have textile experts realised that there is a massive potential to be unlocked from this humble plant.

Jute–the Fibre

Botanically jute comes from one of two closely aligned plants, Corchorus capsularis and C.olitorius. The former has a spherical fruit, flattened at the top and is the species cultivated in Central and East Bengal. The latter has an elongated fruit and is cultivated around Calcutta. Historically both species have grown in the wild in China. The genus Chorchorus grows in many warm, wet countries of the world. In Asia, Africa and America C.olitorius is also called Jewis Mallow and is used as a vegetable in Syria and Egypt. Because of its wide geographical spread it is difficult to determine exactly where the plant originated.

Jute is known as a bast fibre, which means that it comes from the stem of the plant. The plant can grow to a height of 2.5 metres and after harvesting the leaves are allowed to drop off the stems before the tough outer bark is softened in water by a process known as retting. This essentially consists of soaking the stalks in water until the bacterial action makes it easy for the fibre embedded in the stem to be separated and harvested. This can be done in any body of water available. In Bengal, Bihar and Orissa, and in Assam, the retting is done in stagnant water. In low-lying areas, the retting is done in flowing water. Slow moving water allows the retting to be done more evenly producing a very soft fibre.

The retting period depends on the thickness of the stem and can vary between 10 and 20 days. The temperature of the water also affects the speed of retting with the process faster in warmer water. When the retting is complete the bundles are stripped of the fibre. A common procedure for this is to take bundles of ten plants and to beat the roots with a stick. The fibres are wrapped around the fingers and jerked loose. The fibre is then further cleaned and hung up to dry. Jute fibres are silky, golden, grey-brown or off-white, with a high tensile strength and a staple length of around 2 metres (compared with cotton's 4 centimetres).

Left:
*Post retted Jute fibre
(Chemically treated)*

Right:
*Jute fabric & bag
prepared with
enzyme treated
fibre*

POST RETTING SAMPLES

TREATED

CONTROL

ENZYME TREATED   RUSSIAN QUALITY SAMPLES   CONTROL

In India jute is grown in the eastern states of West Bengal, Orissa and Bihar as well as the north eastern states of Assam, Tripura and Meghalaya. An inferior form of jute, known as Mesta, is grown in the southern state of Andhra Pradesh while the states of Madhya Pradesh, Maharashtra and Uttar Pradesh, produce small amounts which are insufficient for industrial exploitation.

However there is an interesting geographical journey involved in jute production. The seeds are grown in the west of India (in the Amaravati district of Maharashtra) in winter, and then brought to the eastern states to be planted in the pre-monsoon period. Attempts have been made to grow enough good seed in the major growing areas, but this has not been successful and the seed's journey across the country continues.

Jute–Its cultivation

Harvested jute
ready for retting

There are strong reasons in the eastern states for beginning jute cultivation during the pre-monsoon showers, which normally come in March or April, and thus having it ready for harvest during the monsoon in July and August. The pre-monsoon showers give sufficient moisture for the germination and growth

of the crop, while the monsoon rains provide ample water in the storage tanks, canals and ditches where the harvested jute is laid to be retted.

Jute has fought off attempts to grow rice in these areas as an alternative crop during this period as it can far better withstand the flooding of fields caused by strong early monsoon showers and recent research shows it to be of a much greater ecological value to the land. It provides natural manure and nutrients to the soil which are of value to the rice, vegetables and other crops which follow jute cultivation. Add to this the biodegradability of jute and it becomes clear that it has a natural and important place in the annual agricultural cycle.

Processing Jute

Rural Jute Processing

In the rural areas of West Bengal and Bihar, as well as in some other states, jute has traditionally been handspun and hand-woven into ropes and rough fabrics. The resulting coarse cloth was used for packaging or covering the body during the cold season. There are records of some poor sections of society using jute for clothing and there is still wide usage of the fibre and yarn for any number of local craft items from toys to wastepaper baskets.

Industrialised Jute Production

With the arrival of the British in the 18th century the need for packaging materials brought jute to the forefront of a new industry to serve the European traders and manufacturers. The growing need to pack and store large quantities of commodities like grains, cereals, potatoes, pulses, salt, oilseeds, cotton and sugar demanded huge quantities of jute bags, which were known in India as gunny bags. Gradually non-edible items like cement, fertiliser and chemicals increased the demand for jute bags.

The packaging material used for these items came to be called sacking material and the jute bags made out of this fabric came to be described as sacks. If the woven structure of the jute fabric was tight and almost non-porous, and thus more suitable for storing and carrying certain materials, it was described as hessian.

And so it was that sacking and hessian rapidly became the hugely dominant percentage of items manufactured in the jute mills and factories, with rope and thread, also used in packaging, making up the rest. Jute was packaging, and packaging was jute! So it remained for approximately a century, underpinned by a market demand which was reacted to by investors and manufacturers by creating more jute for more packaging but never imagining it could have other uses.

Positioning the Industry

India's jute industry became centred around Calcutta as it stood at the heart of a then undivided Bengal (comprising present-day Bangladesh and the Indian state of West Bengal). With mills on either side of the River Hooghly, the jute could be brought from all over the major production area of the Ganges delta, processed into sacking and either used in the port of Calcutta or shipped from there all over the world. This geographical proximity of producer, processing industry and market was convenient, kept costs low and provided the British Empire with a cheap but valuable export product. This situation similarly militated against developing any diversity in the use of jute and for decades this stable but ultimately counter-productive situation remained.

The crises came from a number of directions but of prime importance was the division of Bengal in 1947 when East Pakistan (formerly East Bengal) became independent from India. With this split more than half of Calcutta's hinterland disappeared and its importance as an industrial centre and as a port went into decline. At approximately the same time the rise of cheap, mass-produced synthetic materials posed the first major challenge to the packaging materials of the jute industry.

The fact that jute has survived at all, and indeed is perhaps now poised to realise its true diversity, is in some ways surprising given its history which has suffered from a shortsightedness which has persistently accompanied and stunted its development.

The Beginnings of New Thinking in Jute

The first attempts at the Research and Development of the Jute industry took place as early as 1937, before the impact of the threats mentioned above. The Indian Jute Research Association set about improving the quality of the material, but all its efforts stayed firmly within the confines of jute as packaging. There were remarkable achievements in improving the quality of the fibre, the yarn and the fabric as needed for sacking and hessian. Although this was in answer to a demand for better packaging materials to meet the needs of new commodities to be carried in the sacks, it is astonishing that this team of research scientists seems never to have considered other uses of this fibre. The very people who could have created new products for a new market stayed firmly within the confines of market demands serving the imperial system.

It was only after Independence that there developed an ethos and a recognition of the need for lateral thinking to take the industry forward and it was only really in the 1980s that significant moves were made and markets found.

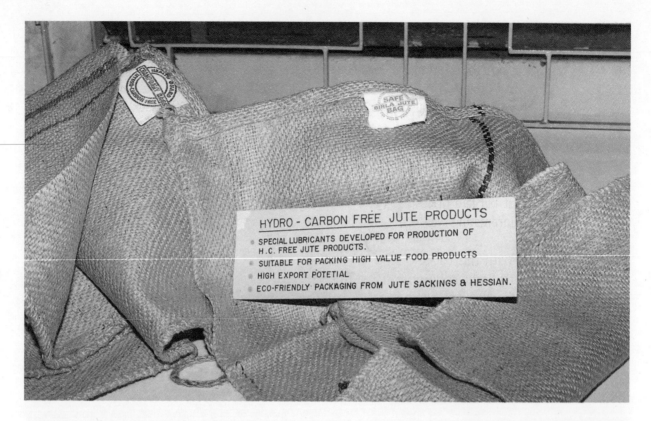

HYDRO - CARBON FREE JUTE PRODUCTS

- SPECIAL LUBRICANTS DEVELOPED FOR PRODUCTION OF H.C. FREE JUTE PRODUCTS.
- SUITABLE FOR PACKING HIGH VALUE FOOD PRODUCTS
- HIGH EXPORT POTETIAL
- ECO-FRIENDLY PACKAGING FROM JUTE SACKINGS & HESSIAN.

New Jute–New Uses

The high tensile strength of jute had always been the main reason for its use in packaging. The same quality led to finding first new markets during the 1980s when it was realised that sacking and hessian made excellent backing material for carpeting and linoleum. At the same time, an accident of economics gave the industry another push forward. Due to rising costs and the introduction of synthetic alternatives, many of Europe's jute mills closed down. The more sophisticated spinning and weaving machinery from these plants was bought at bargain prices by Indian mills and soon finer yarn, lighter fabrics and more interesting weaves became available.

With this background, the Ministry of Textiles took up the challenge in 1987 to find a solution for the future of the jute industry. The primitive, low value machinery, which had traditionally produced the packaging material, clearly could not meet the needs of the end of the twentieth century. Two of jute's original customers, the cement and fertiliser industries, threw up the challenge to produce a more acceptable packaging than that which was being offered by the petroleum industry with its technically superior and highly competitive synthetic bags of high density polyethylene and polypropylene.

Two facts quickly became evident. The first was that unless the jute bags could be technically modified to prevent seepage as much as the synthetic bags, there was no guarantee of a continuing market for jute bags from the cement and fertilizer industry. However much this technical question troubled the policymakers in the Ministry of Textiles, no satisfactory solution seemed to emerge.

*Opposite page
Top:
Hydro-carbon free
Jute bag*

*Bottom:
Traditional filling
of 50 kg. Jute sugar
bags*

The other fact was that there was no way in which jute could guarantee competitive costs. Being an agricultural product jute was highly labour intensive with fluctuations on prices from year to year. In competition with the by-product of a huge and growing petro-chemical industry jute could only be more expensive.

The jute industry was about to lose a substantial part of its market!

The Atira study

Unless the technical problems could be solved the protection of jute farmers and of the industry itself could not be guaranteed as a packaging war threatened. The Ahmedabad Textile Industry Research Association (ATIRA) was therefore requested to carry out a study on the feasibility of producing a blended jute-synthetic material, which would allow both industries to continue to function without conflict. The study would test whether such bags would be cheaper than traditional jute bags, and whether the strengths and weaknesses of each material could be studied in such a way as to produce a better end product.

The response of the petrochemical industry to this study was lukewarm but the findings of the study marked a major shift in conceptualising jute's future. The major points can be summarised as follows:

- Jute, like any other textile fibre, can be 'tamed' and disciplined for many different end-uses.
- Instead of staying bound by the thinking that a jute-synthetic mix would be for packaging purposes only, the industry should realise there were other potential uses in the manufacture of soft luggage, floor coverings and much more.
- Even though a jute-synthetic mix could secure the market for cement and fertiliser, jute value would remain low until textile applications other than packaging were developed. This could bring about an immediate jump in the potential income to the industry.
- New technologies were needed to create new and better uses for jute. Such technology and appropriate new machinery were the key to development and would allow jute to be seen as a textile rather than as packaging.

The ATIRA study made it abundantly clear that the jute industry had to head for diversification. Suddenly it seemed unimaginative in the extreme that the different Textile Research Associations (TRA's) across the country had not been consulted and their expertise tapped for new ideas and technologies. Clearly there was a new place for jute but this would only be achievable if considerable research and development were carried out and considerable cross fertilisation of ideas were to take place between the many jute-related scientists, researchers and artisans across the country.

Handloom Weavers Show the Way

In July 1990 a new initiative in South India blazed a trail for jute's future. The Indian Jute Industries' Research Association together with PSG College of Technology in Coimbatore worked with the local handloom weavers cooperatives to kickstart the use of jute yarn in the handloom sector. Handloom weavers were persuaded to produce floor coverings and furnishings using jute in combination with cotton and viscose yarns.

Left:
Preparation of Jute blended cut-pile carpet on handloom

Right:
Finishing of Jute blended cut-pile carpet prepared in the handloom sector

The results in Chennimilai and Coimbatore were overwhelming. There was a realisation that the delay, indeed the failure, in bringing jute to the highly commercially motivated textile centres of South India had been a huge loss for the jute producers. Immediately the National Textile Corporation (NTC) in Tamil Nadu and the South Indian Textile Research Association (SITRA) were persuaded to look into all the possibilities of using jute.

After the exciting developments of the Ahmedabad report and the Coimbatore trials, efforts were directed towards the possibility of blending jute with wool.

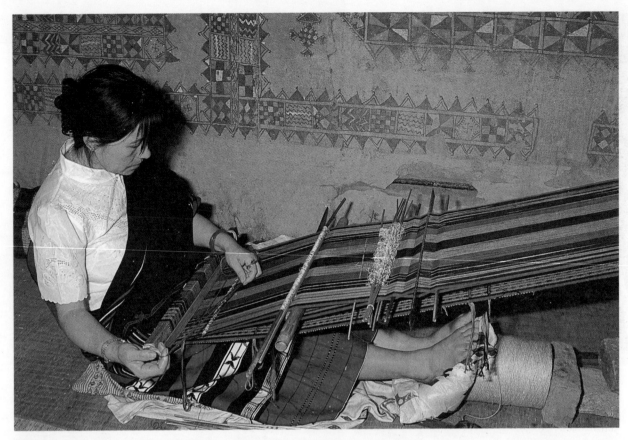

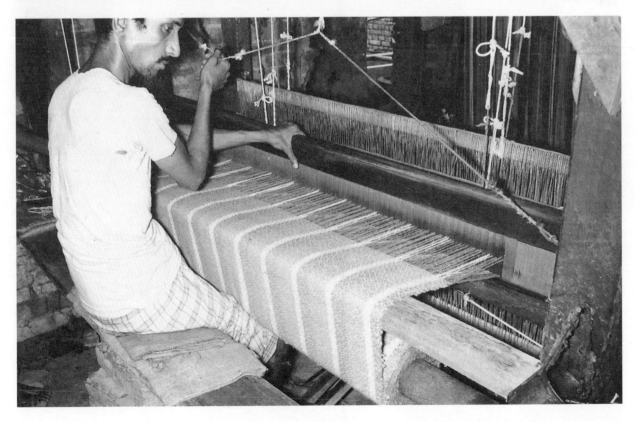

Left:
An interesting jute
furnishing fabric
getting ready on the
loom

Right:
Blending of jute
and rayon fibres
on finisher card

Opposite page
Top:
Jute on the loin
loom

Bottom:
Preparation of jute
blended decorative
fabric on handloom

Working with the Western Research Association (WRA) in Thane, it was quickly realised that there is a great affinity between wool and jute, and if properly blended the new properties of the resulting textile could give rise to many new market possibilities.

With the Bombay Textile Research Association trials were put in place to add dimensional stability for clothing and other effects for drapery and furnishings. Jute was beginning to be seen as having a multitude of uses, and as such the potential to become a truly important textile.

Bringing in the Textile Research Associations to cooperate with IJIRA in the development of new products and the evolving of new technologies conveyed its own signal to the jute industry and these Indian Government initiatives could be seen to have a long-term advantage for other jute producing countries as well as the importing countries willing to experiment with this fibre on the new lines India had mapped out.

Setbacks

These important advances were initially met with staunch resistance from the jute industry. The Jute Research and Development representatives challenged the benefits to be derived by introducing jute to other regions and textile institutions as in this process the jute industry would be deprived of the fibre for its own manufacturing needs. They were of the view that their mandate was to concentrate upon Research and Development related only to those products with which the industry was familiar and which enjoyed established markets, even if these markets were shrinking.

A major section of the industry, unconvinced by the prospects of diversification, solidly stonewalled any move by ministry officials and well-motivated scientists to introduce value-added products to the industry. Endless arguments were raised to denigrate the importance and significance of value-added jute products and a motivated campaign was launched through IJMA to deride diversification as if it were a governmental anti-industry policy. Since IJIRA is technically under the umbrella of the jute industry, although more than 95% of its working funds flow from the Ministry, indirect pressure was put on this institution to refrain from 'hair-brained' ideas and projects relating to jute diversification and concentrate upon traditional products which constituted the bulk of the market.

The rumour was also spread that undertaking research work related to various textile and non-textile products would lose deprive IJIRA of its importance as a premier institution and the jute industry would be the ultimate loser in the bargain. Many of the scientists of IJIRA were also rightly or wrongly under the impression that bringing them in closer cooperation with other TRAs or exposing themselves to the activities of these institutions would jeopardize their importance or dilute their identity.

In spite of this Luddite tendency the fact remained that the historical isolation of jute from other textiles was over in the minds of a sufficient number of scientists, weavers and designers. The cooperation of the Jute research and the textile research bodies finally led to a recognition that jute is an all-India fibre and its challenges should be taken up on a much wider consultative scale than before. Barriers which had existed for decades were finally breached.

Now there is a body of knowledge on jute and its potential which are of national and international importance. And through working with weavers as well as scientists this knowledge was now not limited to the academic sphere, but had been tested and experienced by a wide range of people.

By the mid-nineties jute was generally accepted by the entrepreneurs and was put on display at the multitude of textile seminars and workshops organised all over the country.

The National Jute Programme

On a purely technical level the National Jute Programme responded to the new thinking with a number of trials to produce finer jute yarn and finer blended yarn with the aim of enabling the diversification of jute's textile applications. The Research and Development initiatives focussed on:

- Ring spinning technology in jute mills to produce jute yarn and blended yarn of 4 lbs. and below.
- Ring spinning technology utilising a cotton spinning system for the production of jute-cotton blends.
- Open ended/rotor system of spinning for production of jute-cotton blends.
- the production of Jute-woolen blends in Dref-2 machines.
- Jute woolen blends in the traditional jute ring spinning system.
- Jute cotton blends in the Dref-3 system for denim items.
- REPCO spinning system for jute/cotton/synthetic blends.

This Yarn Technology Mission, as it could be called, had achieved the overall objective of demonstrating to jute mills as well as the textile industry that jute can be spun finer and in attractive blends for different markets and consumer needs.

As a further spin-off, the work gave the industry the impetus to indigenise some of the imported technologies and machineries for meeting the requirements of Indian jute mills as well as textile mills interested in jute yarn production.

Moreover the textile industry was forced to become aware that jute could be bleached, dyed, printed and treated to unleash a new world of possibilities, far removed from its traditional humble role, and a new breed of small and medium-scale entrepreneurs was enthusiastically proving the point.

The role of the handloom exponents in transmitting the message of jute was obvious and well utilised. They explained that jute lends itself beautifully to a number of designs and colour schemes and these could be woven beautifully on handlooms with only minor modifications to the looms. They arranged for training of groups of weavers in the utilisation of jute yarn and explained to them the benefits of jute fabric for furnishing, wall covering, floor covering and other applications.

Close on the heels of developments in the handloom sector, the powerloom industry has also started using jute yarn. Without much Government support, powerloom weavers of Tamil Nadu, West Bengal, Assam, Delhi, Panipat, Ludhiana and other centres have started using jute yarn on powerlooms either in blends with cotton, viscose, wool and polyester yarn, or using jute yarn as the weft in weaving other fibres. Because the output of the powerloom trade is substantially higher than handloom this has made a major difference in the demand for the raw materials.

The groundwork has been done. The weaving sectors have led the way, based on the experimentation and convictions of the Research and Development Institutions. They in turn have ensured public exposure through exhibitions and seminars and have published technical manuals explaining the features of jute and jute blended fabrics and the scope for bleaching, dyeing, printing, ornamentation, stitching, patterning and other uses.

Today jute has revealed its diverse possibilities. Trial ventures have established its feasibility and suitability in many exciting areas:

Jute in Medicines

Ancient Indian texts like Rajnighantu and Bhabaprakosh indicate that different parts of the jute plant were traditionally used to cure a variety of ailments. The bitter leaves of the plants have been used to cure problems in the stomach, intestines and liver. The flowers were used all over South East Asia to cure nasal disorders and the root to stop diarrhoea. Dried leaves made into a brew cure intestinal worms, skin diseases and dysentery. Other concoctions cure jaundice and dermatitis. With a global regeneration of interest into natural remedies and Ayurveda, the medicinal possibilities of jute also hold out an exciting future.

Jute in Handicrafts

This is almost the most traditional use of the fibre after packaging, but new developments have given jute handicrafts a boost. The new yarns and new qualities developed by the industry have immensely broadened the types of handicrafts a skilled artisan can envision and create with this material. At the same time Indian handicrafts in general have gained a substantial foothold in the world market. Now jute can be transformed into a multitude of shapes. Dolls or table mats, lampshades or baskets, hammocks or belts, wall hangings or children's toys—all these and more benefit from the new colours and textures available today.

Opposite page
Top:
Jute based beach/
namaz mats

Bottom:
Jute/acrylic based
carpets

Across the country more and more people are being trained in the manufacture of handicrafts with jute. In Bhopal, for example, some 2,000 women, mostly gas

tragedy victims, now make a reasonable living having been trained in these skills. Across the country voluntary organisations and NGOs are running skills training for disadvantaged and rural workers to join this small, but significant industry, and the National Centre for Jute Diversification aids this process by supplying materials through regional yarn banks.

Jute in Home Furnishings

Ever since jute began its diversification, on the backs of carpets to strengthen them, furnishings seems to have been a natural area for expansion. The marriage of new weights of cloth and strong design have made jute interior furnishings dynamic and affordable. Curtains and cushion covers, chair and sofa coverings, rugs and carpets, tablecloths, room dividers and wallpaper all benefit from a natural appearance with strong textures. It is cheaper than linen, which it resembles in many ways and suits the contemporary taste for ecologically responsible materials. Whether in its own plain colours or in indigo-dyed or highly decorated forms, jute furnishings have a potential to be amongst the most stunning of any textile.

Jute based furnishing fabrics

Jute in Accessories

As the international consumer becomes more and more conscious of the pollution caused by non-biodegradable materials like plastics, jute has been a natural favourite for simple shopping bags. When good designers follow this concept there is no end to the number of handbags, shoulder bags, beach bags and travel bags which can be created from this material. Versions of toilet bags and wash bags, small storage boxes, fashion belts and even shoes are possible from this newly versatile material.

Extreme right:
Flexible jute bag

Right:
Printing of Jute fabric for shoppping/carry bags

Bottom:
Jute bags for school children

Jute in Fashion

In 1990, the first Jute Fashion Show was organised in Delhi. It was a tremendous motivator for young designers and fashion houses as well as the industry. The following decade has seen numerous advances and experiments and jute has certainly claimed a place in the fashion scene, whether in rustic skirts, facings for saris, high fashion jackets or in a thousand other forms. Although all-jute fashion displays are still seen in India and across the world the real success is that jute can be found in normal fashion boutiques alongside other textiles.

The research institutes have developed new treatments to enhance the manner in which the fabric drapes, or how it feels and these advances have improved its commercial viability. Its natural tendency to look like linen is an advantage, especially as it is much cheaper, but it can be spun and woven in so many forms that it could soon appear alongside high quality cottons, silks and fine wool as a luxury item. Fashion is still the real goal for the advancement of jute. If it can really become a commonly used textile its image as only a rough sacking will have gone forever.

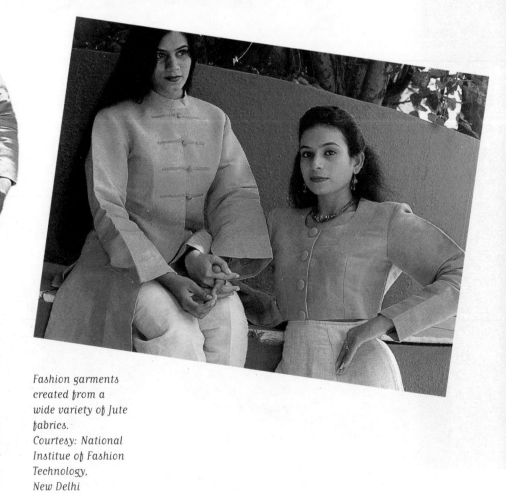

Fashion garments created from a wide variety of Jute fabrics.
Courtesy: National Institue of Fashion Technology, New Delhi

Fashion garment collections by HImanshu Dogra & Dhruti Desai, Sunita Shanker, Upasana & Runna

*Models:
Sonal Valand,
Niyati Shah,
Shyamoli Shah and
Anandi Perumal of
Drapana Academy,
Ahmedabad*

Jute in Ecology

Jute Geo-textile used in gardens and forestry for control of soil erosion.

A fascinating lateral development in jute is not to make it finer, but to make it even more open meshed with thicker yarn. In this net-like form it can be laid on hillsides, valley slopes or railway cuttings to prevent soil erosion and land slippage. Plants grow through it and help bind it in position and it has impressive success rates in preventing one of the most worrying results of deforestation— the washing away of topsoil during heavy rains. It is cheap, environmentally friendly and readily available.

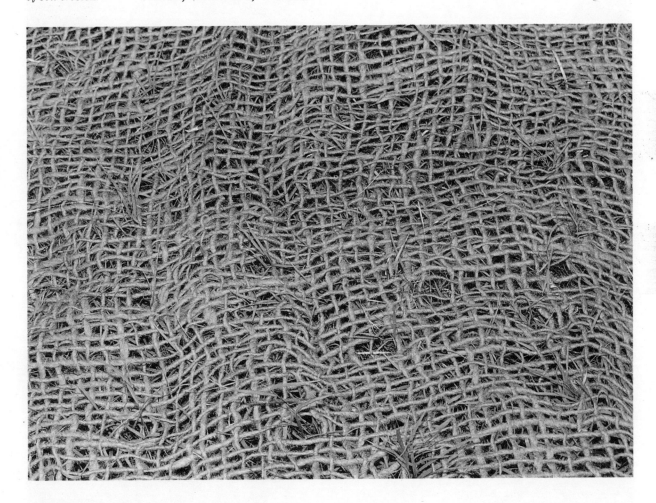

Jute in Board

Impressive results have come from attempts to make composite board of varying types from jute fibre. It can take the place of the glass in glass fibre with huge cost reductions. It can replace wood in pressed particleboard and has even been used to make furniture and door frames. It is a simple concept where jute fibre, in various forms, is held in place as the strengthening material by a resin or glue.

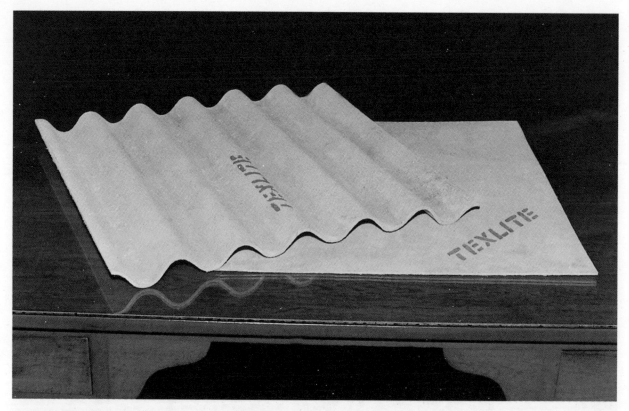

Jute in Paper

Some beautiful articles have been made from bleached jute pulp fashioned into
paper boxes, bags and files. The same strength which made jute suitable for
sacking remains in these items which have not yet become common in the
market, but as an alternative to the diminishing raw materials from which
paper is normally made, jute could soon be of great importance in this area.

*Jute fabric covered
files and folders*

Opposite page
*Top:
Inorganic bonded
Jute composite
boards—plain
and corrugated*

*Bottom:
Decorative Jute stick
particle board*

COLOUR PLATES

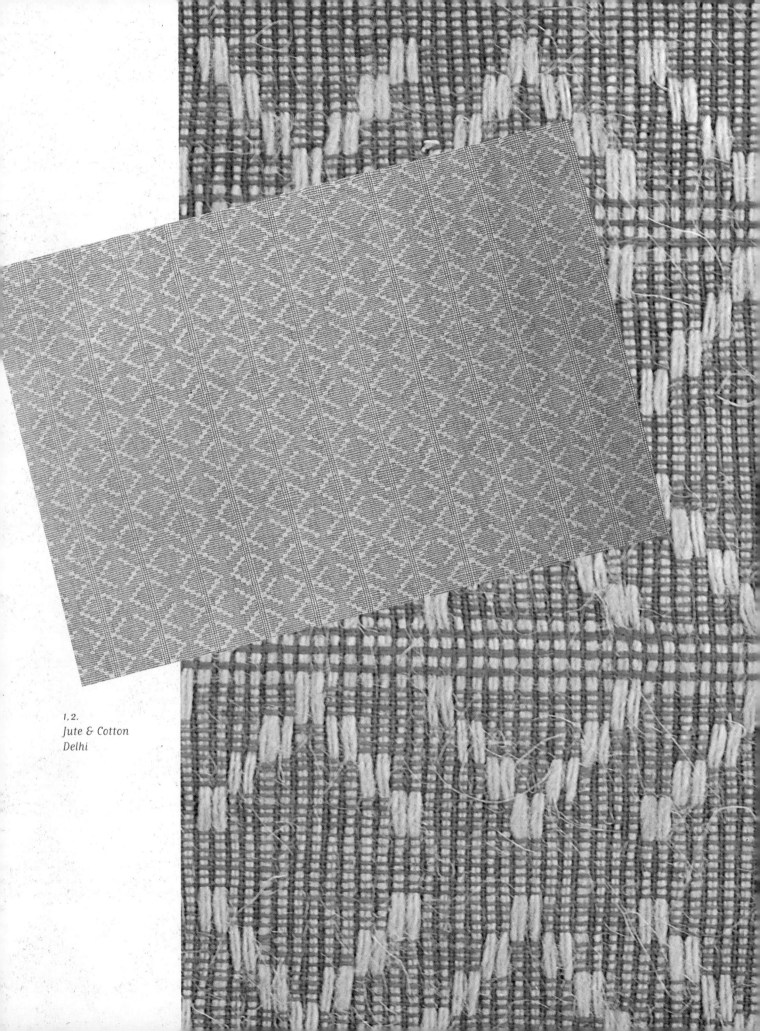

1, 2.
Jute & Cotton
Delhi

3.4.
Cotton & Jute Fabric
Delhi

Opposite page
Top:
5.
Cotton & Jute Fabric
Delhi

Bottom:
6.
Jute & Cotton Fabric
Delhi

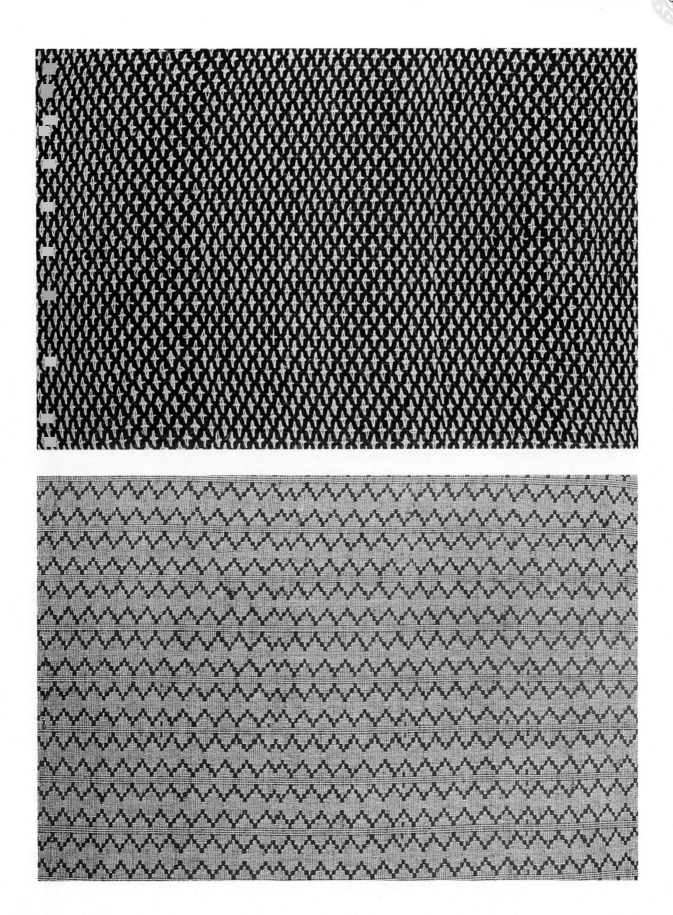

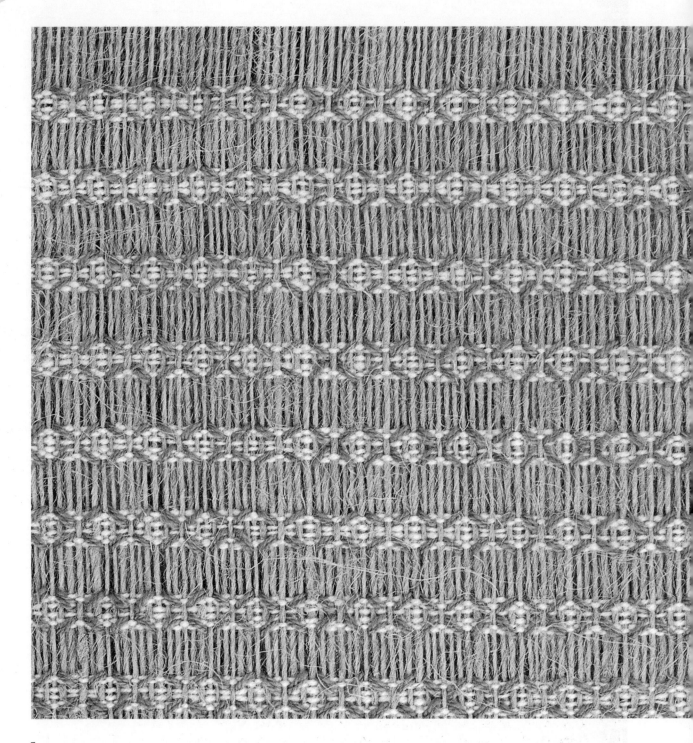

7.
Jute & Cotton Fabric
Delhi

Opposite page
8.
Jute & Cotton
Delhi

Opposite page
9.
Jute & Cotton Fabric
Delhi

10.
Jute & Cotton mat
Delhi

40

11,12.
Jute Fabric
Delhi

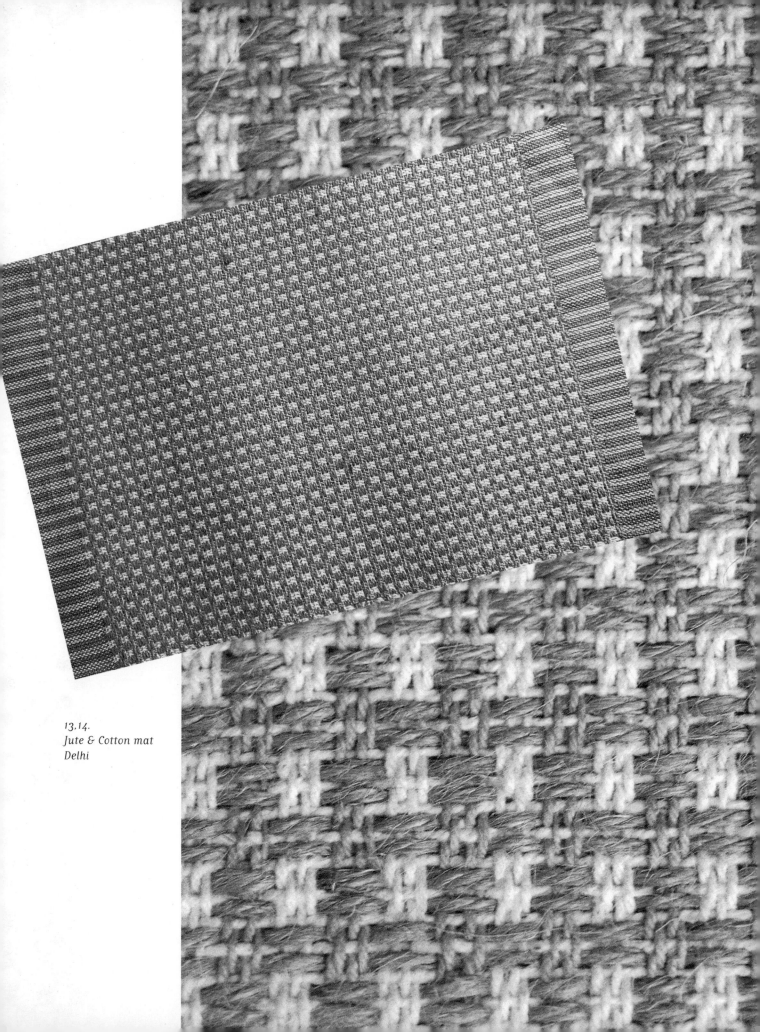

13,14.
Jute & Cotton mat
Delhi

Left:
15.
Jute & Cotton Fabric
Delhi

Centre:
16.
Jute & Cotton mat
Delhi

Right:
17.
Jute & Cotton Fabric
Delhi

18.
Jute mat
Delhi

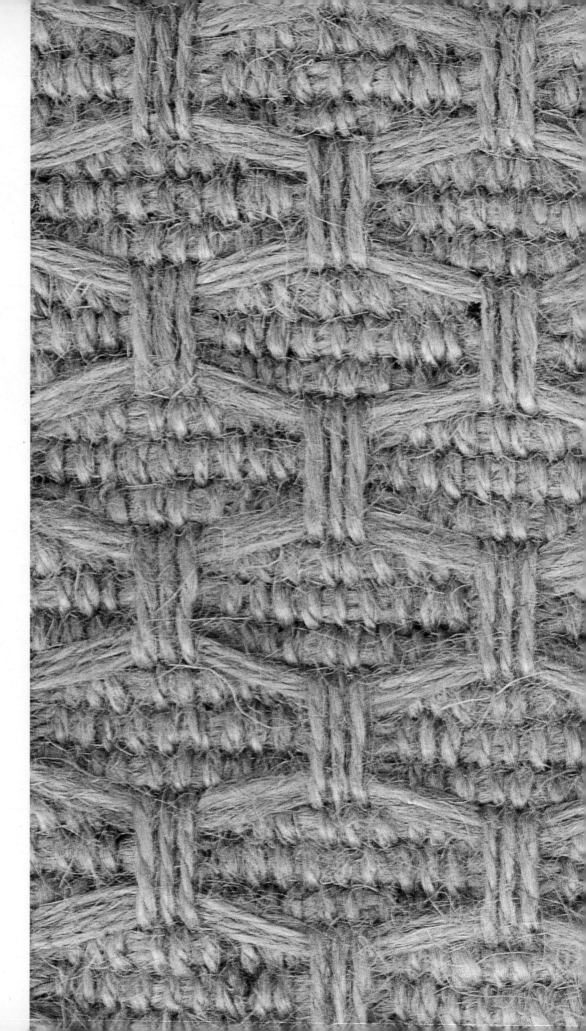

19.
Jute Durry
Delhi

Following page
20.
Jute mat
Delhi

Opposite page
21.
Jute & Cotton Fabric
Delhi

22.
Jute & Cotton Fabric
Delhi

23.
Jute Durry
Delhi

Opposite page
24.
Jute Durry
Delhi

25.
Jute & Cotton Durry
Delhi

Opposite page
26.
Jute & Cotton Durry
Delhi

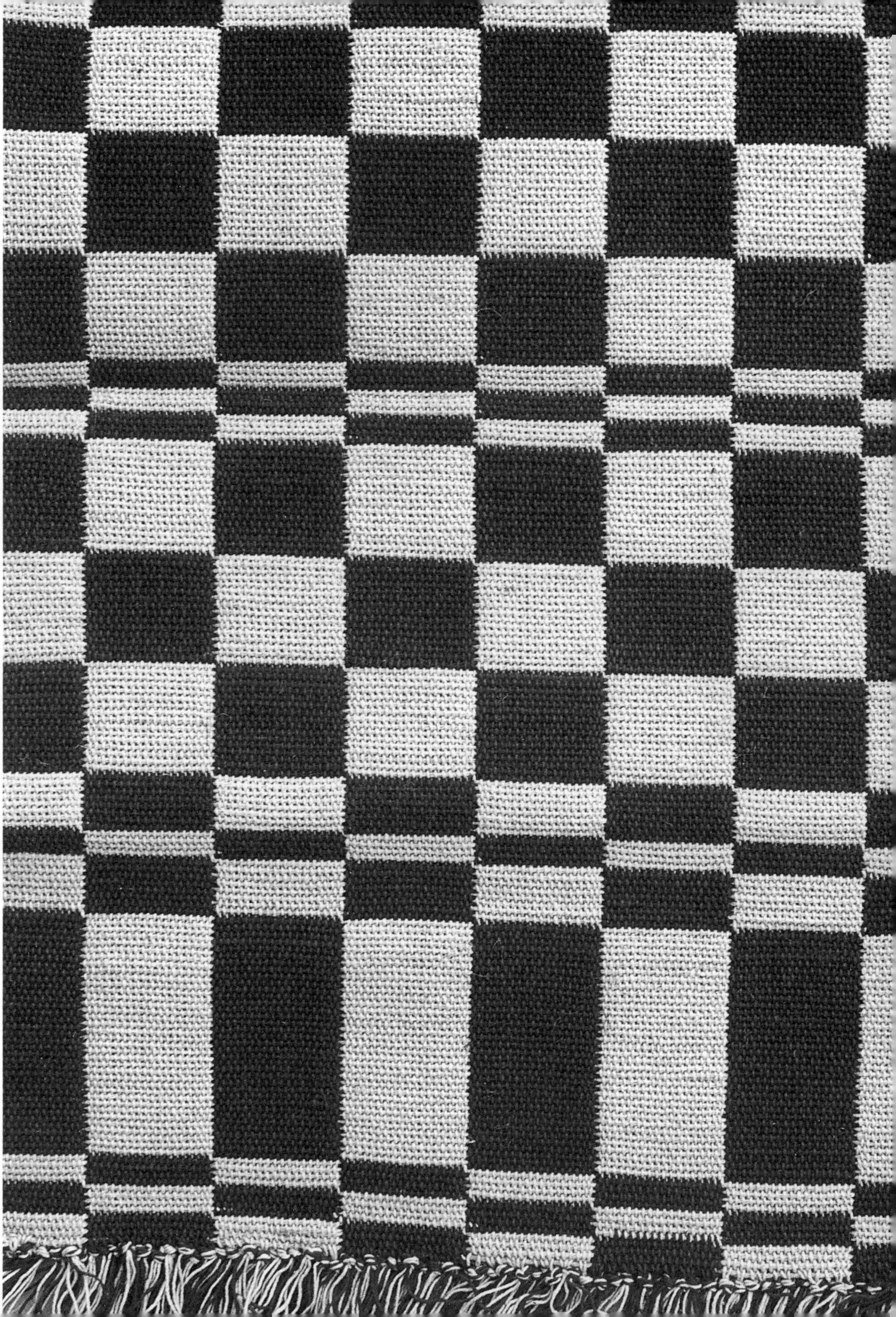

27.
Jute & Cotton Durry
Delhi

28, 29.
*Jute & Cotton Durry
(double cloth)
Delhi*

30, 31.
Jute & Cotton Durry
Delhi

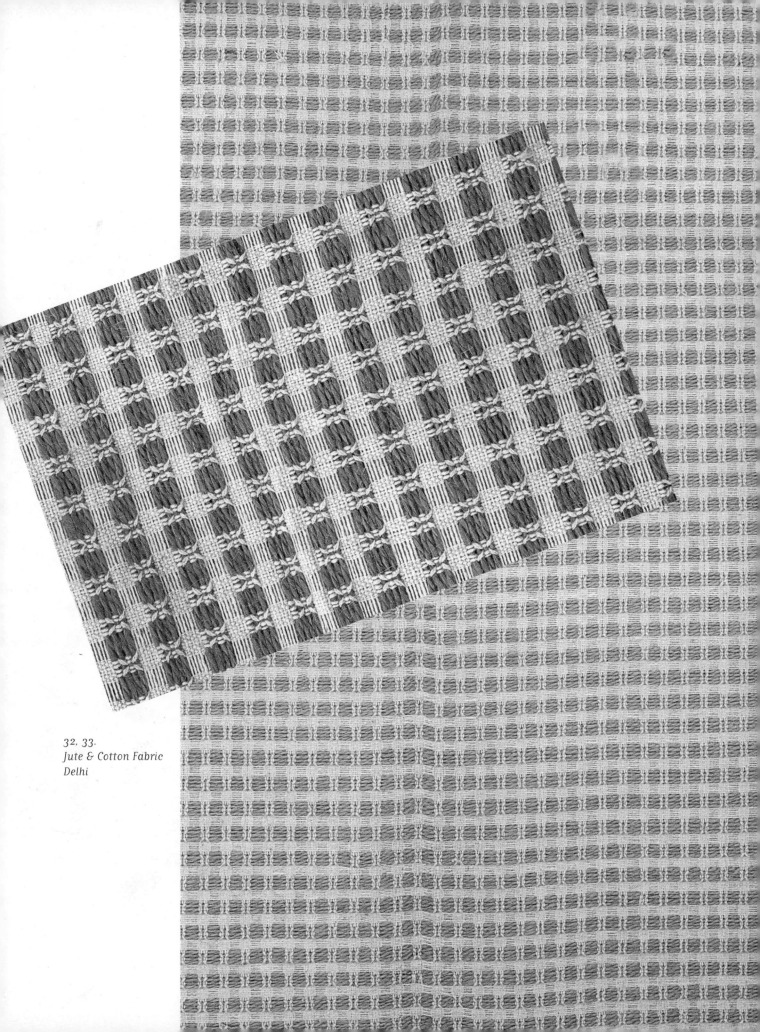

32, 33.
Jute & Cotton Fabric
Delhi

34.
Jute & Cotton Fabric
Delhi

35.
Jute & Cotton Fabric
Delhi

36.
Jute & Cotton Durry
Delhi

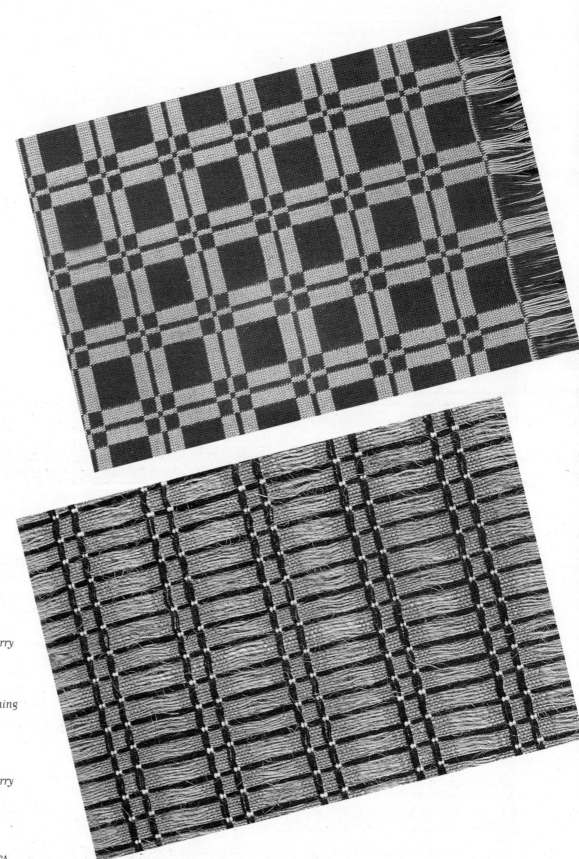

37.
Jute & Cotton Durry
Delhi

38.
Jacquard Furnishing
Tamilnadu

Opposite page
39.
Jute & Cotton Durry
Delhi

Following page
40.
Furnishing Fabrics

Opposite page
41.
Jute Furnishing
Kannur

42.
Jute Viscose Fabric

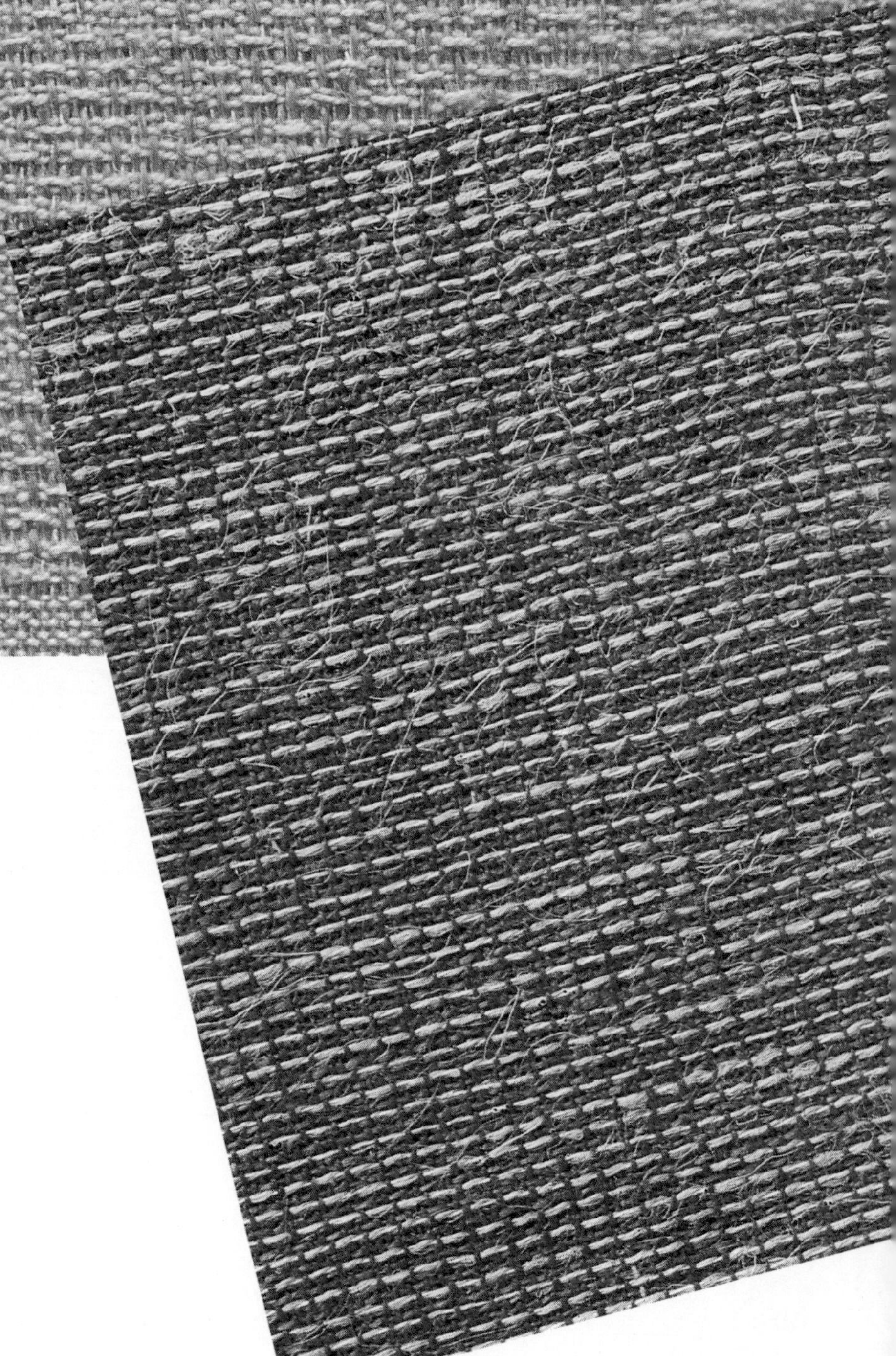

43.
Jute Curtain
Kannur

44.
Jute Viscose Fabric

45.
Jute Furnishing
Kannur

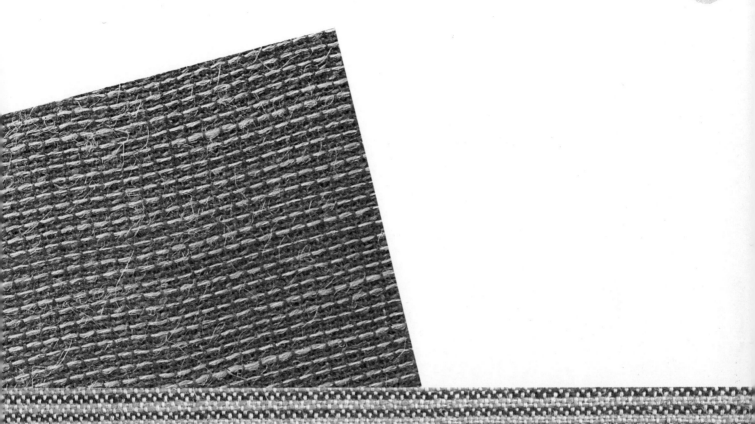

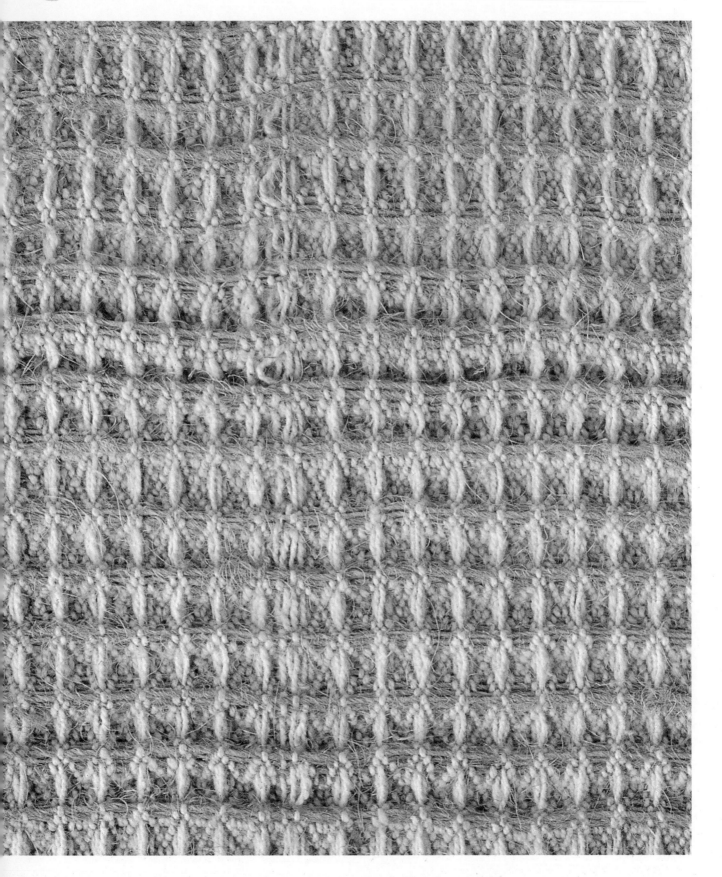

48.
Jute Furnishing
Kannur

49.
Jute Furnishing
Kannur

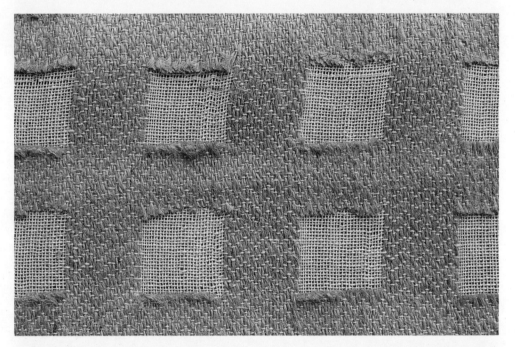

54.
Nadia

55.
Nadia

56.
Nadia

57.
Jute mat
Ghorawal,
Sonebhadra

58.
Small Durry

59.
Furnishings
Tamilnadu

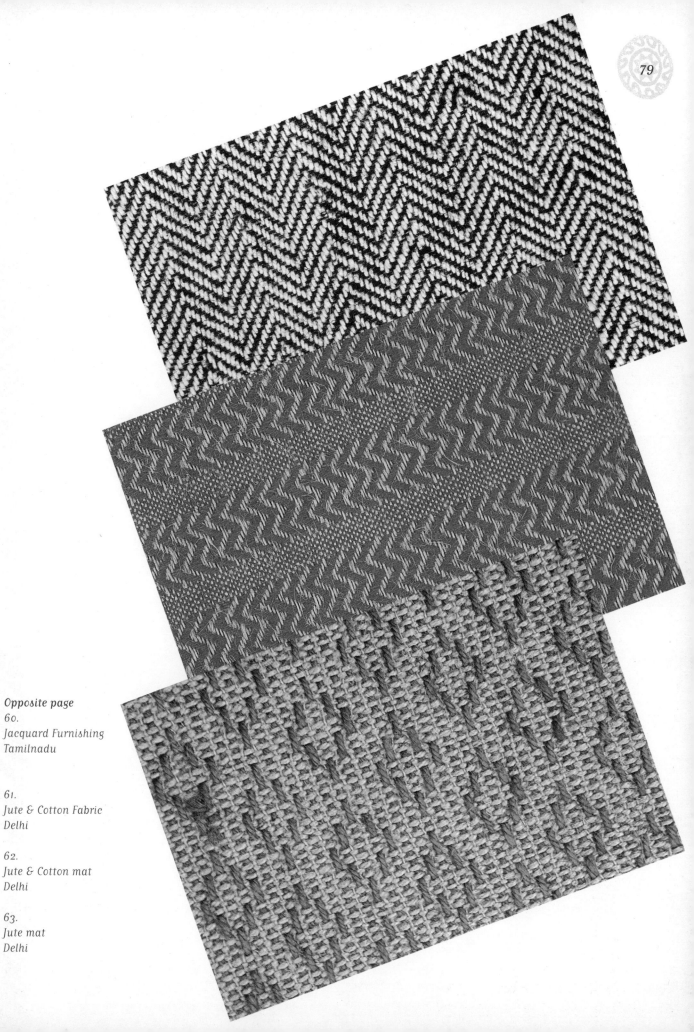

Opposite page
60.
Jacquard Furnishing
Tamilnadu

61.
Jute & Cotton Fabric
Delhi

62.
Jute & Cotton mat
Delhi

63.
Jute mat
Delhi

Opposite page
Top:
64.
Jute & Cotton Fabric
Delhi

Bottom:
65.
Jute Fabric
Delhi

66.
Door mat

Following page
67.
Jute Furnishing
Kannur

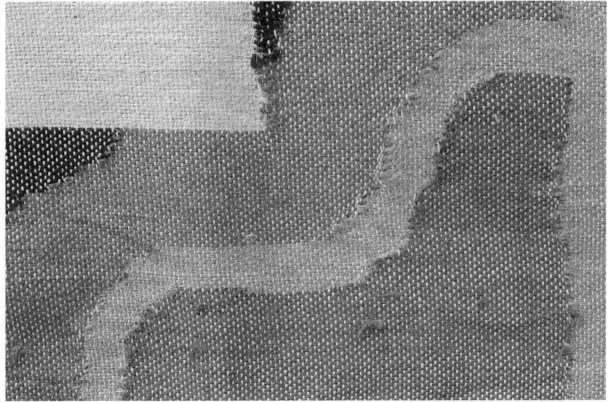

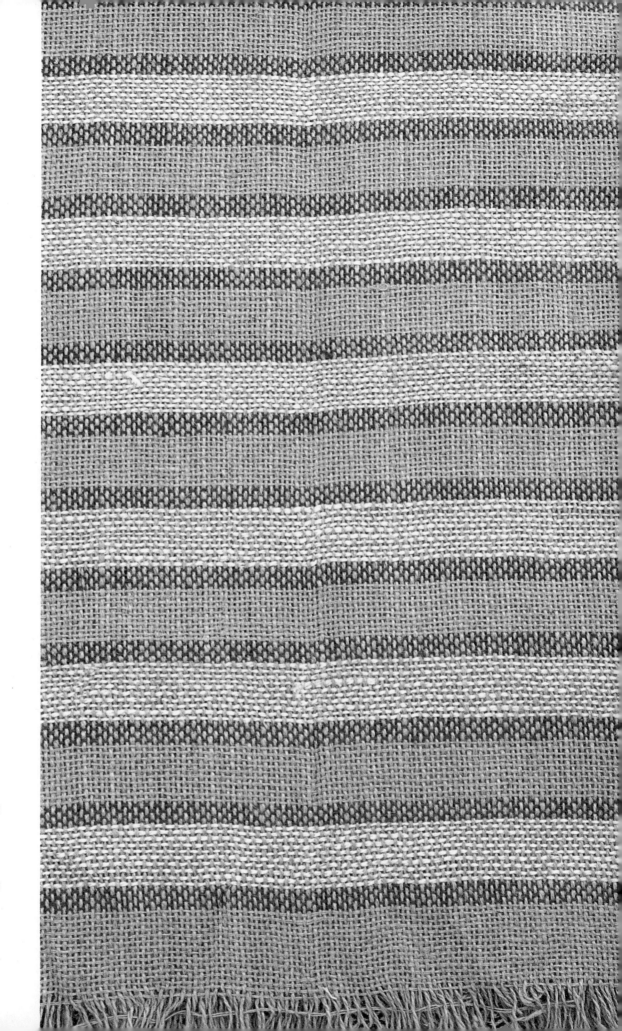

71.
Jute Furnishing
Kannur

Opposite page
Top:
74.
Jute Furnishing
Kannur

Bottom:
75.
Jute Furnishing
Kannur

76.
Floor spread

Following page
77.
Nadia

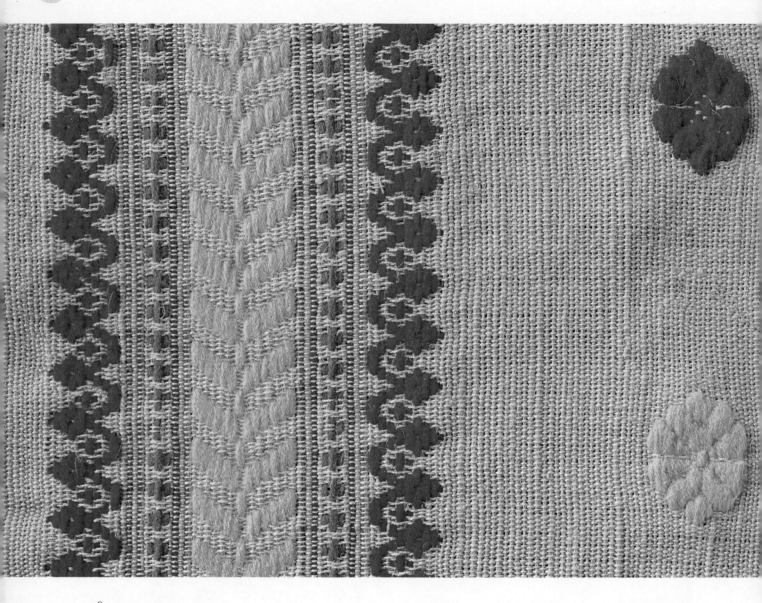

78.
Table Centre mat

Opposite page
79.
Table Centre mat

Previous page
80.
Jute Fabric
Calcutta

81.
Furnishing Fabric
Calcutta

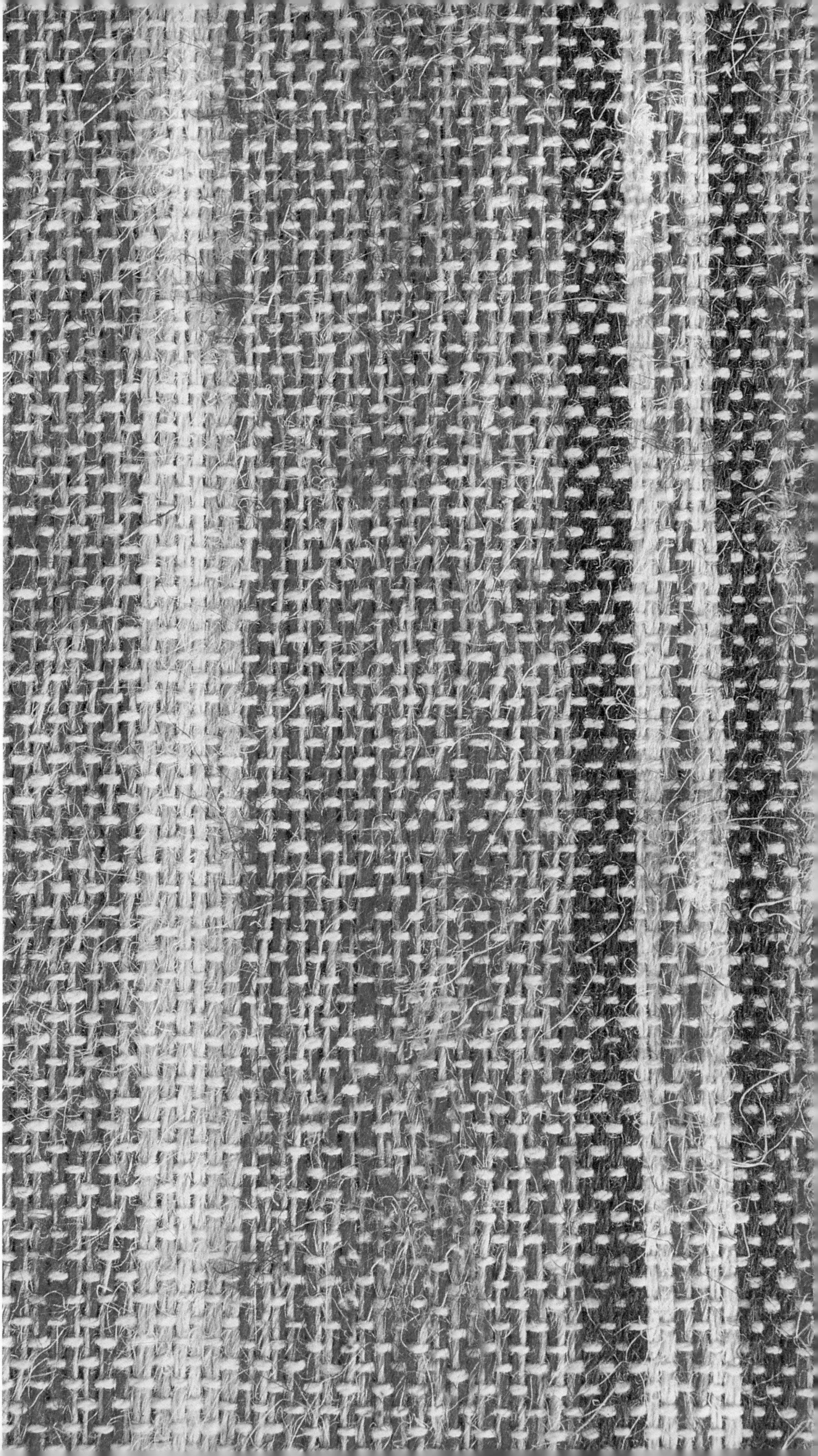

Opposite page
Top:
82.
Jute Fabric
Calcutta

Bottom:
83.
Juco Fabric
Calcutta

84.
Furnishing Fabric

Opposite page
85.
Yardage/Dress
material

86.
Export carpets
Warangal

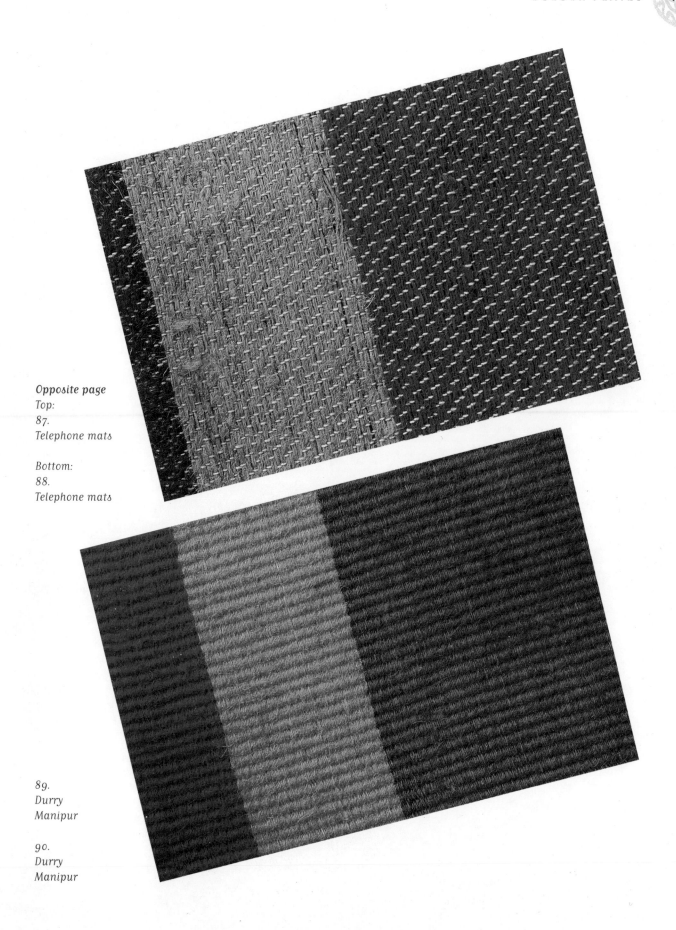

Opposite page
Top:
87.
Telephone mats

Bottom:
88.
Telephone mats

89.
Durry
Manipur

90.
Durry
Manipur

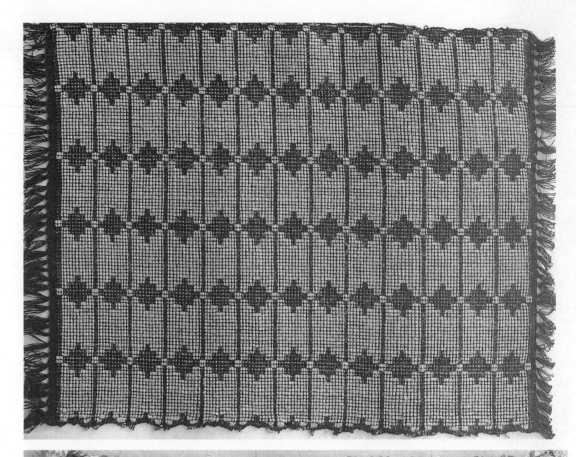

93.
Jute & Cotton mat
Delhi

94.
Jute & Cotton mat
Delhi

Opposite page
95.
Jute mat
Mirzapur

APPENDIX

Appendix I

1, 2.
Jute & Cotton
Puja Handloom, Handicrafts &
Garments, Delhi

Warp : Cotton yarn 2/20
Weft   : Jute and cotton yarn,
             9.5 single ply,
             2/20 cotton
Weave : Plain with extra weft
Reed   : 36
Weight : 500 gms./sq.m.
Ends   : 36/inch
Width : 48 inches

5.
Cotton & Jute Fabric
Puja Handloom, Handicrafts &
Garments, Delhi

Warp   : Cotton yarn 2/20
Weft   : Jute and cotton yarn,
               6 single ply,
               6/2 jute
Weave : Plain with extra warp
               and extra weft
Reed   : 34
Weight : 400 gms./sq.m.
Ends   : 34/inch
Width   : 48 inches

7.
Jute & Cotton Fabric
Puja Handloom, Handicrafts &
Garments, Delhi

Warp   : Cotton yarn 2/20
Weft   : Jute and cotton yarn,
               8 single ply,
               2/20 cotton
Weave : Plain with extra warp
               and *jali*
Reed   : 20
Weight : 300 gms./sq.m.
Ends   : 20/inch
Width   : 48 inches

3, 4.
Cotton & Jute Fabric
Puja Handloom, Handicrafts &
Garments, Delhi

Warp   : 2/10
Weft   : Jute yarn,
              9.5 pound 2 ply,
              2/20 cotton
Weave : Plain with extra weft
Reed   : 24
Weight : 550 gms./sq.m.
Ends   : 24/inch
Width : 54 inches

6.
Jute & Cotton Fabric
Puja Handloom, Handicrafts &
Garments, Delhi

Warp   : Cotton yarn 2/30
Weft   : Jute and cotton yarn,
               9.5 single ply,
               2/20 jute and cotton
Weave : Plain with extra weft
Reed   : 36
Weight : 450 gms./sq.m.
Ends   : 36/inch
Width   : 48 inches

8.
Jute & Cotton
Puja Handloom, Handicrafts &
Garments, Delhi

Warp   : Cotton yarn 2/40
Weft   : Jute and cotton yarn,
               9.5 single ply,
               2/20 Cotton
Weave : Plain with extra weft
Reed   : 40
Weight : 500 gms./sq.m.
Ends   : 40/inch
Width   : 48 inches

9.
Jute & Cotton Fabric
Puja Handloom, Handicrafts &
Garments, Delhi

Warp : Cotton yarn 2/20
Weft : Jute yarn,
4.5 pound
Weave : Plain with design
Reed : 48
Weight : 400 gms./sq.m.
Ends : 48/inch
Width : 48 inches

10.
Jute & Cotton mat
Puja Handloom, Handicrafts &
Garments, Delhi

Warp : Jute and cotton mix
2/20
Weft : Jute yarn,
8 pound
Weave : Plain with design
Reed : 24
Weight : 100 gms. (13 x 18)
Ends : 24/inch
Width : 13 inches

11,12.
Jute Fabric
Puja Handloom, Handicrafts &
Garments, Delhi

Warp : 9.5 pound 2 ply
Weft : Jute yarn,
9.5 pound 2 ply
Weave : Plain check
Reed : 16
Weight : 700 gms./sq.m.
Ends : 16/inch
Width : 48 inches

13,14.
Jute & Cotton mat
Puja Handloom, Handicrafts &
Garments, Delhi

Warp : 3/6 cotton
Weft : Jute and cotton yarn,
11 pound 3 single ply,
13/6 cotton
Weave : Plain pick by pick
Reed : 16
Weight : 125 gms./sq.m.
Ends : 16/inch
Width : 14 inches

15.
Jute & Cotton Fabric
Puja Handloom, Handicrafts &
Garments, Delhi

Warp : 2/20 cotton
Weft : Jute yarn,
8 pound Jute
Weave : Diamond
Reed : 48
Weight : 600 gms./sq.m.
Ends : 48/inch
Width : N/A

16.
Jute & Cotton mat
Puja Handloom, Handicrafts &
Garments, Delhi

Warp : 3/6 cotton yarn
Weft : Jute yarn,
9.5 pound 2 ply
Weave : Matt weave
Reed : 16
Weight : 150 gms. (14 x 18)
Ends : 16/inch
Width : 14 inches

17.
Jute & Cotton Fabric
Puja Handloom, Handicrafts &
Garments, Delhi

Warp : 2/20
Weft : Jute yarn,
4.5 single ply,
2/20 jute
Weave : Twill with plain
Reed : 48
Weight : 450 gms./sq.m.
Ends : 48/inch
Width : 48 inches

18.
Jute mat
Puja Handloom, Handicrafts &
Garments, Delhi

Warp : 9.5 pound 2 ply
Weft : Jute yarn,
11 pound 3 ply
Weave : Diamond
Reed : 10
Weight : 100 gms. (13 x 18)
Ends : 10/inch
Width : 13 inches

19.
Jute Durry
Puja Handloom, Handicrafts &
Garments, Delhi

Warp : 9.5 pound 2 ply
Weft : Jute yarn,
14 pound 3 ply
Weave : Plain with extra warp
Reed : 16
Weight : 800 gms. (2 x 3)
Ends : 16/inch
Width : 24 inches

20.
Jute mat
Puja Handloom, Handicrafts &
Garments, Delhi

Warp   : 9.5 pound 2 ply
Weft   : Jute yarn,
             14 pound 3 ply,
             4.5 pound Jute
Weave : Plain with extra weft
Reed   : 10
Weight : 90 gms. (13 x 18)
Ends   : 10/inch
Width : 13 inches

21.
Jute and Cotton Fabric
Puja Handloom, Handicrafts &
Garments, Delhi

Warp   : 2/20 cotton
Weft   : Jute yarn and cotton
             2/20 cotton 9.5 pound
             2 ply
Weave : Plain with extra weft
Reed   : 40
Weight : 450 gms./sq.m.
Ends   : 40/inch
Width : 48 inches

22.
Jute and Cotton Fabric
Puja Handloom, Handicrafts &
Garments, Delhi

Warp   : 2/30 cotton
Weft   : Jute fancy yarn,
Weave : Plain
Reed   : 40
Weight : 600 gms./sq.m.
Ends   : 40/inch
Width : 48 inches

23.
Jute Durry
Puja Handloom, Handicrafts &
Garments, Delhi

Warp   : 9.5 pound 2 ply
Weft   : Jute yarn,
             14 pound 3 ply
Weave : Satin and sateen weave
Reed   : 20
Weight : 3 kgs. (4 x 6)
Ends   : 20/inch
Width : 48 inches

24.
Jute Durry
Puja Handloom, Handicrafts &
Garments, Delhi

Warp   : 9.5 pound 2 ply
Weft   : Jute yarn,
             14 pound 3 ply
Weave : Twill
Reed   : 16
Weight : 700 gms. (2 x 3)
Ends   : 16/inch
Width : 24 inches

25.
Jute and Cotton Durry
Puja Handloom, Handicrafts &
Garments, Delhi

Warp   : 3/6 double cloth
Weft   : Jute yarn,
             14 pound 3 ply
Weave : Double cloth
Reed   : 16
Weight : 900 gms. (2 x 3)
Ends   : 16/inch
Width : 24 inches

26.
Jute & Cotton Durry
Puja Handloom, Handicrafts &
Garments, Delhi

Warp   : 3/6 double cloth
Weft   : Jute yarn,
             14 pound 3 ply
Weave : Double cloth
Reed   : 16
Weight : 900 gms. (2 x 3)
Ends   : 16/inch
Width : 24 inches

27.
Jute & Cotton Durry
Puja Handloom, Handicrafts &
Garments, Delhi

Warp   : 3/6
Weft   : Jute yarn,
             14 pound 3 ply
Weave : Double cloth
Reed   : 16
Weight : 900 gms. (2 x 3)
Ends   : 16/inch
Width : 24 inches

28, 29.
Jute & Cotton Durry
(double cloth)
Puja Handloom, Handicrafts &
Garments, Delhi

Warp   : 3/6 cotton
Weft   : Jute yarn,
             14 pound 3 ply
Weave : Double cloth
Reed   : 16
Weight : 900 gms. (2 x 3)
Ends   : 16/inch
Width : 24 inches

30, 31.
Jute & Cotton Durry
Puja Handloom, Handicrafts &
Garments, Delhi

Warp	: 3/6 double cloth
Weft	: Jute yarn, 14 pound 3 ply
Weave	: Double cloth
Reed	: 16
Weight	: 3.200 kgs. (4 x 6)
Ends	: 16/inch
Width	: 48 inches

32, 33.
Jute & Cotton Fabric
Puja Handloom, Handicrafts &
Garments, Delhi

Warp	: 2/20
Weft	: Jute yarn, 2/10
Weave	: Plain with *jali* (extra warp)
Reed	: 16
Weight	: 450 gms./sq.m.
Ends	: 16/inch
Width	: 54 inches

34.
Jute & Cotton Fabric
Puja Handloom, Handicrafts &
Garments, Delhi

Warp	: 2/20 cotton
Weft	: Jute yarn, 8 pound jute
Weave	: Diamond
Reed	: 48
Weight	: 600 gms./sq.m.
Ends	: 48/inch
Width	: 48 inches

35.
Jute & Cotton Fabric
Puja Handloom, Handicrafts &
Garments, Delhi

Warp	: 2/20 cotton
Weft	: Jute yarn, 8 pound jute
Weave	: Plain
Reed	: 24
Weight	: 600 gms./sq.m.
Ends	: 24/inch
Width	: 48 inches

36.
Jute & Cotton Durry
Puja Handloom, Handicrafts &
Garments, Delhi

Warp	: 3/6 cotton
Weft	: Jute yarn, 14 pound, 3 ply jute
Weave	: Double cloth
Reed	: 16
Weight	: 900 gms. (2 x 3)
Ends	: 16/inch
Width	: 24 inches

37.
Jute & Cotton Durry
Puja Handloom, Handicrafts &
Garments, Delhi

Warp	: 3/6 cotton
Weft	: Jute yarn, 14 pound, 3 ply Jute
Weave	: Double cloth
Reed	: 16
Weight	: 900 gms. (2 x 3)
Ends	: 16/inch
Width	: 24 inches

38.
Jacquard Furnishing
The Chennimalai Industrial
Weavers Co-op.
Production & Sale Society Ltd,
Tamilnadu

Warp	: 2/17 cotton
Weft	: 6s Jute
Weave	: Plain and float
Reed	: N/A
Weight	: 400 gms./sq.m.
Ends	: 40/inch
Width	: 36 inches

39.
Jute & Cotton Durry
Puja Handloom, Handicrafts &
Garments, Delhi

Warp	: 3/6 cotton and jute 9.5 pound 2 ply
Weft	: Jute yarn, 14 pound 3 ply
Weave	: Plain with extra warp
Reed	: 16
Weight	: 700 gms. (2 x 3)
Ends	: 16/inch
Width	: 24 inches

40.
Furnishing Fabrics

Warp	: Cotton
Weft	: Jute
Peddles	: 6
Weave	: N/A
Reed	: 4
Weight	: N/A
Ends	: N/A
Width	: N/A

41.

Jute Furnishing

The Kanhirode Weavers' Co-op.
P & S Society Ltd., Kannur

Warp   : 2/17
Weft   : 3.8 lbs. J/V
Weave : Jacquard
Reed   : 56
Weight : 330 gms./sq.m.
P P   : 32/inch
Width : 50 inches

42.

Jute Viscose Fabric

Warp   : 3.2 lbs. jute
Weft   : 3.8 lbs. jute
Weave : N/A
Reed   : 30
Weight : 250 gms./sq.m.
Ends   : 28/inch
Width : N/A

43.

Jute Curtain

The Kanhirode Weavers' Co-op.
P & S Society Ltd., Kannur

Warp   : 2/17
Weft   : 3.8 lbs. Jute
Weave : Plain and mockleno
Reed   : 36
Weight : 300 gms./sq.m.
Picks : 36/inches
Width : 48 inches

44.

Jute Viscose Fabric

Warp   : 20/2 cotton
Weft   : 3.8 lbs. jute viscose
Weave : N/A
Reed   : 30
Weight : 250 gms./sq.m.
Ends   : 28/inch
Width : N/A

45.

Jute Furnishing

The Kanhirode Weavers' Co-op.
P & S Society Ltd., Kannur

Warp   : 2/40 (2 ply)
Weft   : 3.8 lbs. J/V
Weave : Plain with extra weft
Reed   : 48
Weight : 452 gms./sq.m.
Ends   : 48/inch
Width : 50 inches

46.

Jute Viscose Fabric

Warp   : 10/3
Weft   : 8 pounds
Weave : N/A
Reed   : 24
Weight : 400 gms./sq.m.
Ends   : 24/inch
Width : N/A

47.

Furnishing Fabric

Warp   : Cotton
Weft   : Jute
Peddles : 6
Weave   : N/A
Reed   : 4
Weight : N/A
Ends   : N/A
Width   : N/A

48.

Jute Furnishing

The Kanhirode Weavers' Co-op.
P & S Society Ltd., Kannur

Warp   : 2/40
Weft   : 3.8 lbs. J/V
Weave : Plain with rib
Reed   : 72
Weight : 270 gms./sq.m.
P P   : 32/inch
Width : 50 inches

49.

Jute Furnishing

The Kanhirode Weavers' Co-op.
P & S Society Ltd., Kannur

Warp   : 2/40
Weft   : 3.8 lbs. J/V
Weave : Plain with rib effect
Reed   : 72
Weight : 265 gms./sq.m.
Ends   : 72/inch
P P   : 32/inch
Width : 50 inches

50.
Furnishing Fabrics

Warp   : Cotton
Weft   : Jute
Peddles : 6
Weave   : N/A
Reed   : 4
Weight : N/A
End   : N/A
Width   : N/A

51.
Cotton Jute Furnishing/ Door curtain

Warp   : 2/17 cotton yarn
Weft   : 6 lbs. jute
Weave : Multi treadle (Twill)
Reed   : 40 (2 in a dent for 8
         dents miss 8 dents)
Weight : 185 gms./sq.m.
Ends   : 32/inch
Width : 52 inches

52.
Jute Furnishing
The Kanhirode Weavers' Co-op.
P & S Society Ltd., Kannur

Warp   : 2/17
Weft   : 3.8 lbs. J/V
Weave : Rib
Reed   : 56
Weight : 378 gms./sq.m.
P P   : 40/inch
Width : 50 inches

53.
Nadia
Ranaghat 1 No. Panchayat
Tapasili Sramik
Tantubay Samabay Samity Ltd.

Warp   : 10/2 cotton
Weft   : 6 lbs. 2 ply natural
         colour
Weave : N/A
Reed   : 20
Weight : 355 gms./sq.m.
         (60% jute, 40% cotton)
End   : Plane
Width : 44 inches

54.
Nadia
Ranaghat 1 No. Panchayat
Tapasili Sramik
Tantubay Samabay Samity Ltd.

Warp   : 10s cotton single
Weft   : 4 lbs. Jute
Weave : N/A
Reed   : 40
Weight : 390 gms./sq.m.
         (50% jute, 50% cotton)
Ends   : N/A
Width : N/A

55.
Nadia
Ranaghat 1 No. Panchayat
Tapasili Sramik
Tantubay Samabay Samity Ltd.

Warp   : 17/2 cotton
Weft   : 4 lbs. 2 ply plus
         17/2 cotton
Weave : Jacquard allovu
Reed   : 20
Weight : 440 gms./sq.m.
         (50% jute, 50% cotton)
End   : N/A
Width : 42 inches

56.
Nadia
Ranaghat 1 No. Panchayat
Tapasili Sramik
Tantubay Samabay Samity Ltd.

Warp   : 10/2 cotton
Weft   : 6 lbs. 3 ply jute
Weave : N/A
Reed   : 24
Weight : 135 gms./sq.m.
         (50% jute, 50% cotton)
Ends   : Dobby design
Width : 22 inches

57.
Jute mat
Ghorawal, Sonebhadra

Warp   : Jute plied yarn
Weft   : Jute plied yarn
Weave : Twill design
Reed   : 6
Weight : 2.700 kgs./sq.m.
Ends   : 6/inch
Width : 18 inches

58.
Small Durry

Warp   : Jute
Weft   : Jute
Weave : N/A
Reed   : N/A
Weight: N/A
End   : N/A
Width : N/A

59.
Furnishings
The Chennimalai Industrial
Weavers Co-op.
Production & Sale Society Ltd.,
Tamilnadu

Warp   : 2/6 cotton
Weft   : 6s Jute
Weave : Broken twill
Reed   : 40
Weight: 625 gms./sq.m.
Ends   : 26/inch
Width : 50 inches

60.
Jacquard Furnishing
The Chennimalai Industrial
Weavers Co-op.
Production & Sale Society Ltd.,
Tamilnadu

Warp   : 2/17
Weft   : 4s jute
Weave : Jacquard
Reed   : 64s
Weight: 400 gms./sq.m.
Ends   : 66/inch
Width : 60 inches

61.
Jute & Cotton Fabric
Puja Handloom, Handicrafts &
Garments, Delhi

Warp   : 2/10 cotton
Weft   : Jute yarn,
         8 pound jute
Weave : Pointed twill
Reed   : 24
Weight: 500 gms./sq.m.
Ends   : 24/inch
Width : 48 inches

62.
Jute & Cotton mat
Puja Handloom, Handicrafts &
Garments, Delhi

Warp   : 2/20 cotton
Weft   : Jute yarn,
         8 pound jute
Weave : Plain with twill pointed
Reed   : 30
Weight: 90 gms./sq.m.
Ends   : 30/inch
Width : 13 x 18 inches

63.
Jute mat
Puja Handloom, Handicrafts &
Garments, Delhi

Warp   : 9.5 pound 2 ply
Weft   : Jute yarn,
         14.3 ply,
         8 pound single
Weave : Plain with extra weft
Reed   : 12
Weight: 100 gms. (13 x 18)
Ends   : 12/inch
Width : 13 inches

64.
Jute & Cotton Fabric
Puja Handloom, Handicrafts &
Garments, Delhi

Warp   : 2/20 cotton
Weft   : Jute yarn,
         8 pound jute
Weave : Plain
Reed   : 36
Weight: 500 gms./sq.m.
Ends   : 36/inch
Width : 48 inches

65.
Jute Fabric
Puja Handloom, Handicrafts &
Garments, Delhi

Warp   : 9.5 pound 2 ply
Weft   : Jute yarn,
         9.5 pound 2 ply
Weave : Plain
Reed   : 12
Weight: 500 gms./sq.m.
Ends   : 12/inch
Width : 48 inches

66.
Door mat

Warp   : 2/20 cotton yarn
Weft   : 10 lbs. jute
Weave : N/A
Reed   : 20
Weight: N/A
Ends   : 20/inch
Width : N/A

67.
Jute Furnishing
The Kanhirode Weavers' Co-op.
P & S Society Ltd., Kannur

Warp   : 2/17
Weft   : 3.8 lbs. J/V
Weave : Plain
Reed   : 36
Weight : 230 gms./sq.m.
Ends   : 36/inch
Width : 48 inches

68.
Jute Furnishing
The Kanhirode Weavers' Co-op.
P & S Society Ltd., Kannur

Warp   : 2/17
Weft   : 3.8 lbs. J/V
Weave : Plain
Reed   : 36
Weight : 230 gms./sq.m.
Ends   : 36/inch
Width : 48 inches

69.
Jute Furnishing

Warp   : 3/6
Weft   : Jute
Weave : N/A
Reed   : 18
Weight : 1.300 kgs./sq.m.
Ends   : N/A
Width : 48 inches

70.
Jute Fabric
Puja Handloom, Handicrafts &
Garments, Delhi

Warp   : 9.5 pound 2 ply
Weft   : Jute yarn,
          8 pound jute single,
          9.5 pound 2 ply jute
Weave : Plain
Reed   : 8
Weight : 500 gms./sq.m.
Ends   : 8/inch
Width : 48 inches

71.
Jute Furnishing
The Kanhirode Weavers' Co-op.
P & S Society Ltd., Kannur

Warp   : 2/17
Weft   : 3.8 lbs. J/V
Weave : Plain with extra weft
Reed   : 48
Weight : 472 gms./sq.m.
Ends   : 48/inch
Width : 50 inches

72.
Union Fabrics

Warp   : 2/20 cotton yarn
Weft   : 10 lbs. jute
Weave : N/A
Reed   : 40
Weight : N/A
Ends   : 40/inch
Width : N/A

73.
Union Fabrics

Warp   : 2/20 cotton yarn
Weft   : 10 lbs. jute
Weave : N/A
Reed   : 40
Weight : N/A
Ends   : 40/inch
Width : N/A

74.
Jute Furnishing
The Kanhirode Weavers' Co-op.
P & S Society Ltd., Kannur

Warp   : 2/30
Weft   : 6 lbs. jute
Weave : Plain
Reed   : 52
Weight : 300 gms./sq.m.
Ends   : 52/inch
Width : 48 inches

75.
Jute Furnishing
The Kanhirode Weavers' Co-op.
P & S Society Ltd., Kannur

Warp   : 2/30
Weft   : 6 lbs. jute
Weave : Plain
Reed   : 52
Weight : 300 gms./sq.m.
Ends   : 52/inch
Width : 48 inches

76.
Floor spread

Warp	: 2/20 cotton yarn
Weft	: 12 lbs. jute
Weave	: N/A
Reed	: 20
Weight	: N/A
Ends	: 20/inch
Width	: N/A

77.
Nadia

Ranaghat 1 No. Panchayat
Tapasili Sramik
Tantubay Samabay Samity Ltd.

Warp	: 17/2 cotton
Weft	: 4 lbs. jute
	natural colour
Weave	: N/A
Reed	: 40
Weight	: 360 gms./sq.m. (60% jute, 40% cotton)
Ends	: N/A
Width	: 50 inches

78.
Table Centre mat

Warp	: 2/20 cotton yarn
Weft	: 4 lbs. jute
Weave	: N/A
Reed	: 40
Weight	: N/A
Ends	: 40/inch
Width	: N/A

79.
Table Centre mat

Warp	: 2/20 cotton yarn
Weft	: 4 lbs. jute
Weave	: N/A
Reed	: 40 inch
Weight	: N/A
Ends	: 40/inch
Width	: N/A

80.
Jute Fabric

Khadi Pratisthan, Calcutta

Warp	: 2/40 cotton
Weft	: 6 lbs./spy jute yarn
Weave	: Plain
Reed	: 40 split per 2 inch
Weight	: 750 gms./sq.m.
Ends	: 40/inch
Width	: 20 inches

81.
Furnishing Fabric

Khadi Pratisthan, Calcutta

Warp	: 2/40 cotton
Weft	: 6 lbs./spy jute
Weave	: Plain
Reed	: 40 split per 2 inch
Weight	: 500 gms./sq.m.
Ends	: 40/inch
Width	: 20 inches

82.
Jute Fabric

Khadi Pratisthan, Calcutta

Warp	: 2/40
Weft	: 8 lbs./spy jute yarn
Weave	: Plain
Reed	: 40 split per 2 inch
Weight	: 710 gms./sq.m.
Ends	: 20/inch
Width	: 20 inches

83.
Juco Fabric

Khadi Pratisthan, Calcutta

Warp	: 2/40 cotton
Weft	: 8 lbs./jute yarn
Weave	: Plain
Reed	: 40 split per 2 inch
Weight	: 725 gms./sq.m.
Ends	: 40/inch
Width	: 20 inches

84.
Furnishing Fabric

Warp	: Cotton
Weft	: Jute
Peddles	: 6
Weave	: N/A
Reed	: 4
Weight	: N/A
Ends	: N/A
Width	: N/A

85.
Yardage/Dress material

Warp : 2/17
Weft : 5 lbs. jute
Weave : N/A
Reed : 36
Weight : 500 gms./sq.m.
Ends : 20/inch
Width : 0.67 mts. width
       2.50 mts. height

86.
Export Carpets
Shatranji & W.W.C.S Ltd.,
Uppu Mallaiah Tbcota
Kothawada, Warangal (AP)

Warp : 3/6 cotton
Weft : Jute 3 ply
Weave : Plain and design
Reed : 8 Ends/1 inch
Weight : 0.120 gms./sq.feet
Ends : 8.1/inch
Width : 24 inches

87.
Telephone mats

Sample size : 23 cm x 27 cm
Warp : Jute
Weft : Jute
Peddles : 4
Weave : N/A
Reed : 4
Weight : N/A
Ends : N/A
Width : N/A

88.
Telephone mats

Warp : Saleen
Weft : Jute
Peddles : 4
Weave : N/A
Reed : 4
Weight : N/A
Ends : N/A
Width : N/A

89.
Durry
Crafts Society of Manipur

Warp : 2/30 cotton
Weft : 6 lbs. jute
Weave : Twill
Reed : 20
Weight : 756.75 gms./sq.m.
Ends : 20/inch
Width : 38 inches

90.
Durry
Crafts Society of Manipur

Warp : 2/6 cotton
Weft : 4 lbs. J/V blend
Weave : Plain
Reed : 16
Weight : 477.97 gms./sq.m.
Ends : 20/inch
Width : 18 inches

91.
Floor spread
Gramin Jan-Kalyan Sansthan,
Mirzapur

Warp : 2/10 cotton
Weft : 8 lbs. jute
Weave : Plain and design
Reed : 16
Weight : 1.900 kgs./sq.m.
Ends : 8/inch
Width : N/A

92.
Export Carpets
(Cotton & Jute)
Shatranji & W.W.C.S Ltd.
Uppu Mallaiah Tbcota
Kothawada, Warangal (AP)

Warp : 3/6 cotton
Weft : Jute 3 ply
Weave : Plain and design
Reed : 8/1
Weight : 0.120 gms./sq.feet
Ends : 8.1/inch
Width : 24 inches

93.
Jute & Cotton mat
Puja Handloom, Handicrafts &
Garments, Delhi

Warp : Cotton yarn 2/20
Weft : Jute and cotton yarn,
       9.5 pound ply,
       2/20 cotton
Weave : Plain pick by pick
Reed : 36
Weight : 90 gms. (13 x 18)
Ends : 36/inch
Width : 13 inches

94.
Jute & Cotton mat
Puja Handloom, Handicrafts &
Garments, Delhi

Warp : 2/4 cotton
Weft : Jute yarn,
          2/4 cotton,
          7 mm. jute fine
Weave : Extra weft with plain
Reed : 16
Weight : 150 gms./sq.m.
Ends : 16/inch
Width : 14 x 18 inches

95.
Jute mat
Gramin Jan-Kalyan Sansthan,
Mirzapur

Warp : 2/4 cotton
Weft : 8 lbs. jute yarn
Weave : Plain
Reed : 16
Weight : 1.100 kgs./sq.m.
Ends : 16/inch
Width : N/A

Appendix II

Select List of Manufacturers

**Shatranji & Handloom Weaver's
Co-op. Society Ltd.**
H. No. 11-25-1149
Kothawada
Warangal
Andhra Pradesh

Assam Co-op Silk House Ltd.
Panbazar
Guwahati 781 001
Assam

**Shri Puja Handloom, Handicrafts
& Garments Co-op. Industrial
Society Ltd.**
559, Moti Ram Road
Shahdara
Delhi 110 032

**Suchitra Women Weavers HL
& HC Society**
ALEO Manali 175 131
District: Kullu
Himachal Pradesh

**The Kanhirode Weavers Co-op
P&S Society Ltd.**
P.O. Kanhirode
Via Koodali
District: Cannanore 670 592
Kerala

Crafts Society of Manipur
Salam Leikai
Sagolband
Imphal 795 001
Manipur

Khudra Weavers Co-op Society Ltd.
P.O. Khudra
At Samantrapur
District: Khudra
Orissa

Sadhana Rural Foundation
13/1, K.K. Road
Saligramam
Chennai 600 093
Tamilnadu

Weavers Service Centre
Chennai
Tamilnadu

**The Chennimalai Industrial
Weavers Co-op. Production &
Sale Society Ltd.**
P.R.S. Road, Chennimalai 638 051
District: Erode
Tamilnadu

Gramin Jan-Kalyan Sansthan
Hayat Nagar
Sabari Natawan Road
Mirzapur 231 001
Uttar Pradesh

Niryatak Handloom Co-op Society
35-A, Shujat Ganj
Kanpur 208 013
Uttar Pradesh

**Shri Shiv Prasad Chaubey &
Samaj Kalyan Bal Vidya Mandir**
Baghel Lane, Welleslyganj
Mirzapur 231 001
Uttar Pradesh

Khadi Pratisthan
15 College Square
Calcutta 700 073
West Bengal

**Ranaghat 1 No. Panchayet
Tapasili Sramik Tantubay Samabay
Simity Ltd.**
Village: Raghabpur, P.O. Panapara
Railway Station, Habibpur
PS Ranaghat
District: Nadia 741 201
West Bengal

Indian Organisations for Development of Jute

Jute Manufacturers Development Council, Ministry of Textiles Government of India

Head Office:
71 Park Street, 3A Park Plaza
Calcutta 700 016
West Bengal
Phone: 033-299240 / 293437 /
          293438 / 293825
Fax: 033-297136
Telex: 021-5677 JMDC IN

Regional Offices:
i) Chenetha Bhawan
    Shop No.4, Nampally
    Hyderabad 500 001
    Andhra Pradesh
    Telefax: 040-4614918

ii) 1203, Nirmal Towers
    26, Barakhambha Road
    New Delhi 110 001
    Phone: 011-3721554

iii) 2, R.K. Mutt Road
     Picnic Plaza, Luz Corner
     Mylapore
     Chennai 600 004
     Tamil Nadu
     Phone: 044-4940908

Association of jute Entrepreneurs of Northern India (AJENI)
21 Community Centre
Friends Colony
New Delhi 110 065
Tel: 011-6837920
Fax: 011-6834890

National Institute of Fashion Technology
NIFT Campus, Hauz Khas
Near Gulmohar Park
New Delhi 110 016
Tel: 011-6965980 / 5059
Fax: 011-6851198

Office of Development Commissioner (Handicrafts)
West Block-7, R K Puram
New Delhi 110 066
Phone: 011-6106902

Office of Development Commissioner (Handlooms)
Ministry of Textiles
Udyog Bhavan
New Delhi 110 011
Phone: 011-3012945
Fax: 011-3792429

Ahmedabad Textile Industry's Research Association
P.O. Ambawadi Vistar
Ahmedabad 380 015
Gujarat
Phone: 079-6302672 / 6304671
Fax: 079-6302874

Association of Jute Entrepreneurs of Western India (AJEWI)
O/O Managing Director
Gujarat Sheep & Wool Development
Corporation Ltd. (GUSHEEL)
Block No.18, 5th Floor
Udyog Bhavan, Sector 11
Gandhinagar 382 011
Gujarat
Tel: 082-31028 / 32254
Fax: 082-29651

The Technological Institute of Textiles & Sciences
Birla Colony
Bhiwani 125 021
Haryana
Phone: 01664-45427
Fax: 01664-43728

Bombay Textile Research Association
Lal Bahadur Shastri Marg
Ghatkopar (West)
Mumbai 400 086
Maharashtra
Phone: 022-5003651 / 5002652
Fax: 022-5000459

India Institute of Packaging
E-2 MIDC AREA
Post Box 9432, Andheri (East)
Mumbai 400 093
Maharashtra
Phone: 022-8219803 / 8216751
Fax: 022-8375302
Telex: 011-79042

Wool Research Association
Akbar Camp Road, P.O. Sandoz Baug
Kolshet Road, Thane
Mumbai 400 607
Maharashtra
Phone: 022-5346453 / 5414284
Fax: 022-5343629

Association of Jute Entrepreneurs of South India (AJESI)
O/O Dept. of Textile Technology
PSG College of Technology
Peelamedu
Coimbatore 641 004
Tamil Nadu
Tel: 0422-572177
Fax: 0422-572069 / 573833

The PSG College of Technology
P.B. No. 1611, Peelamedu
Coimbatore 641 004
Tamil Nadu
Phone: 0422-572177 / 572069
Fax: 0422-573833

The South India Textile Research Association
P.O. Coimbatore Aerodrome
Coimbatore 641 014
Tamil Nadu
Phone: 0422-574010
Fax: 0422-571896

Northern India Textiles Research Association
Sector-23, Rajnagar
Ghaziabad 201 002
Uttar Pradesh
Phone: 0575-721785 / 722858
Fax: 0575-721796

Central Pulp and Paper Research Institute
Star Paper Mill Road
Saharanpur 247 001
Uttar Pradesh
Phone: 0132-727227 / 727036

Association of Jute Entrepreneurs
of Eastern India (AJEEI)

Association for Development
of Jute and Allied Composites
O/O NCJD
ICMARD Building (8th Floor)
Block 14, CIT Scheme VIII(M)
Ultadanga
Calcutta 700 067
West Bengal
Tel: 033-3563269/3563373
Fax: 033-3513270

Bureau of Indian Standards
1/14, C I T Scheme VII M
VIP Road, Manicktola
Calcutta 700 054
West Bengal
Tel: 033-3558298
Fax: 033-3557459

Calcutta Jute Fabrics Shippers
Association
4, India Exchange Place (7th Floor)
Calcutta 700 001
West Bengal
Tel: 033-2207763
Fax: 033-2203973

Central Research Institute for
Jute & Allied Fibres Indian
Council of Agricultural Research
Barrackpore 743 101
24-Parganas (North)
West Bengal
Phone: 5600849
Telex: 021-4091

The Directorate of Jute
Development, Ministry of
Agriculture, Government of India
234/4, A J C Bose Road
Calcutta 700 020
West Bengal
Phone: 033-2479465
Cable: DIRJUTE

The East India Jute and
Hessian Exchange Ltd.
43, Netaji Subhas Road
Calcutta 700 001
West Bengal
Tel: 033-2206118

Electronics Research and
Development Centre
WEBEL Bhavan
Block-EP & GP
Sector V, Bidhannagar
Calcutta 700 091
West Bengal
Tel: 033-2352651
Fax: 033-2354562

Export Inspection Council
Ministry of Commerce
Government of India
14/1B, Ezra Street
Calcutta 700 001
West Bengal
Phone: 033-252651
Telex: 021-4431

Gunny Trades Association
5, Dr. Rajendra Prasad Sarani
Calcutta 700 001
West Bengal
Tel: 033-2203233

Indian Jute Industries'
Research Association
17, Taratola Road
Calcutta 700 088
West Bengal
Phone: 033-4784615
Fax: 033-4784621
Telex: 021-8141

Indian Jute Mills Association
6, Netaji Subhas Road
Calcutta 700 001
West Bengal
Phone: 033-2209918
Fax: 033-2205643
Telex: 021-7369 BCCI IN

Institute of Jute Technology
35, Ballygunge Circular Road
Calcutta 700 019
West Bengal
Phone: 033-4751985
Fax: 033-4750996

The Jute Balers Association
12 India Exchange Place
Calcutta 700 001
West Bengal
Tel: 033-2202805

The Jute Corporation of India Ltd.
1, Shakespeare Sarani
Calcutta 700 071
West Bengal
Phone: 033-2828831
Telex: 021-3266

Jute Technological Research
Laboratories Indian Council
of Agricultural Research
12, Regent Park
Calcutta 700 040
West Bengal
Phone: 033-4710192
Fax: 033-4712583
Telex: 021-2966 JTRL IN

The Legan Jute Machinery Co. Ltd.
24B, Park Street
Calcutta 700 016
West Bengal
Phone: 033-299665
Fax: 033-292169
Telex: 021-5960

National Centre for Jute
Diversification
ICMARD Building (8th Floor)
Blcok 14, CIT Scheme VIII (M)
Ultadanga
Calcutta 700 067
West Bengal
Fax: 0132-727387

National Institute of Research
on Jute and Allied Fibre
Technology
Indian Council of Agricultural
Research
12, Regent Park
Calcutta 700 040
West Bengal
Tel: 033-4710192
Fax: 033-4712583

National Jute Manufacturers
Corporation Ltd.
Chartered Bank Buildings
4, Netaji Subhas Road
Calcutta 700 001
West Bengal
Phone: 033-2206121
Fax: 033-2205103
Telex: 021-7439

North Bengal Jute Farmers
and Entrepreneurs Association
Sudarsanpur (North)
Raiganj 733 134
Uttar Dinajpur
West Bengal
Tel: 03525-53368
Fax: 03523-52602

Office of Jute Commissioner
Ministry of Textiles
Government of India
20B, Abdul Hamid Street
Calcutta 700 069
West Bengal
Phone: 033-2486451
Fax: 033-2489658
Telex: 021-7865

The State Trading Corporation
of India Ltd.
11, R N Mukherjee Road
Calcutta 700 001
West Bengal
Tel: 033-2202494
Fax: 033-2488165

Raw Material Banks

Andhra Pradesh
**Hyderabad Institute of
Fashion Technology**
D3, Huda Complex, Tarnaka
Hyderabad 500 007
Phone: 040-7019527
Fax: 040-7017930

Orugallu Dhurries Manufacturers
H.No. 11-25-1177, Kothawada
Warrangal 506 012
Phone: 08712-25103
Fax: 08712-24677

Sai Karan Handlooms
H. No. 11-25-589, Kothawada
Warrangal 506 012 (A.P.)

Assam
Siddha Products Pvt. Ltd.
S.R.C.B. Road, Fancy Bazar
Guwahati 781 001
Phone: 0361-544577
Fax: 0361-544577

Gujarat
H. R. International Limited
1st Floor, Krishna Mansion
Ghee Bazar, Kalupur
Ahmedabad 380 002

Haryana
Blended Commercial
1118, New Housing Board Colony
Uttar Panipat (Haryana)

Manipur
Rural Service Agency
Imphal 795 001
Manipur Palace Compound (West)
Phone: 0385-223145
Fax: 0385-222936

New Delhi
Runak International
150/11 Shiv Ashram
S P Mukherjee Marg
Delhi 110 006

Orissa
**The Agricultural Promotion
and Investment Corporation
of Orissa Ltd.**
1266, Unit-IX
Bhubaneshwar 751 007
Phone: 0674-420525/420506
Fax: 0674-420506

Punjab
Harjit Singh & Sons
Chowk Mallah Singh Majith Mandi
Amritsar 143 006
Phone: 0183-54408, 552366
Fax: 0183-552366

Rahul Commercial Combine
148, Industrial Area
Near Cheema Chowk
Ludhiana 1410 03
Phone: 0161-550604/5556353
Fax: 0161-5591653

Tamil Nadu
Mankind Manoeuvres
(Karicore Creation Unit)
54/1, Police Commissioner
Office Road, Egmore
Chennai 600 008
Phone: 044-8231603
Fax: 044-8251328

Uttar Pradesh
A T R Commercial Corporation
117/K/109, R S Puram,
Sarvodaya Nagar
Kanpur 208 025 (U.P.)
Phone: 0512-213871/72
Fax: 0512-547613

West Bengal
Eastern Juwool Tex Pvt. Ltd.
Issam Banerjee Lane, Jaganath Tala
Nabadwip

Mangalam
Dharsha Brahman Para
P S Jagacha Howrah

Marketing & Research Centre
86, B R B Bose Road
(Canning Street) 2nd Floor
Calcutta 700 001
Phone: 033-251468
Fax: 033-2253990/2254275

Saroda Textile
25, G T Road Baidyabati
Hooghly
Calcutta 712 222
Phone: 033-632247

Siddha Products Pvt. Ltd.
78, Hazra Road
Calcutta 700 029
Phone: 033-4746374/4764445

Regional Directors' Office

The Regional Director (NER)
O/O the Development
Commissioner (Handicrafts)
Kalyanpur, Ganeshpuri
Guwahati 781 006
Assam

The Regional Director (NR)
O/O the Development
Commissioner (Handicrafts)
West Block No. 8
R K Puram
New Delhi 110 066

The Regional Director (WR)
O/O the Development
Commissioner (Handicrafts)
Haroon House, 3rd Floor
294, P Nariman Street, Fort
Mumbai 400 001
Maharashtra

The Regional Director (SR)
O/O the Development
Commissioner (Handicrafts)
Shastri Bhawan
3rd Floor
26 Haddows Road
Chennai 600 006
Tamil Nadu

The Regional Director (CR)
O/O the Development
Commissioner (Handicrafts)
Government of India
Ministry of Textiles
B-46, (J Park)
Mahanagar Extension
Lucknow 226 006
Uttar Pradesh

The Regional Director (ER)
O/O the Development
Commissioner (Handicrafts)
3rd Floor, DF- Block
Salt Lake City
Calcutta 700 064
West Bengal

Design Centres of the Office of Development Commissioners (Handicrafts)

The Dy. Director
O/O The Development
Commissioner (Handicrafts)
Regional Design & Technical
Development Centre
43, Okhla Industrial Estate
New Delhi 110 020

The Dy. Director
O/O The Development
Commissioner (Handicrafts)
Regional Design & Technical
Development Centre (DW)
No.78 Church Street
Bangalore 560 001
Karnataka

The Dy. Director
O/O The Development
Commissioner (Handicrafts)
Regional Design & Technical
Development Centre (TW)
32, Victoria Road
Bangalore 560 047
Karnataka

The Dy. Director
O/O The Development
Commissioner (Handicrafts)
Regional Design & Technical
Development Centre
Sitaram Mill Compound
Municipal School, 3rd Floor
Ramji Boricha Marg
Mumbai 400 011
Maharashtra

The Dy. Director
O/O The Development
Commissioner (Handicrafts)
Regional Design & Technical
Development Centre
9/12, Old Court House Street
Calcutta 700 002
West Bengal

Bibliography

ATIRA. *Third Workshop and Exhibition on Jute: The Golden Fibre.* Ahmedabad, Ahmedabad Textile Industry's Research Association, 1996

Goswami, Omkar. *Industry, Trade, and Peasant Society: The Jute Economy of Eastern India, 1900–1947.* New Delhi, Oxford University Press, 1991.

Ghosh, G K. *Ecofriendly Development with Jute.* New Delhi, Ashish Publishing House, 1994

Indian Jute Industries' Research Association: Golden Jubilee (1937–1987). Calcutta, 1988

Saptharishi, L V. *Indian Jute: Vision of the Future.* New Delhi, Contact Communications, 1996

ATIRA. *Techno-Economic Feasibility Studies for Producing Jute/Jute Blended Yarns.* Ahmedabad, Ahmedabad Textile Industry's Research Association, 1997

JMDC. *Productivity Norms for The Jute Industry.* Calcutta, Jute Manufacturers Development Council, 1978

ATIRA. *Second Workshop and Exhibition on Jute: The Golden Fibre.* Ahmedabad, Ahmedabad Textile Industry's Research Association, 1994

Goyal, H D. *Indian Jute Industry: Problems and Prospects.* New Delhi, Commonwealth Publishers, 1990

JMDC. *Indian Jute, Vol VIII No.2.* Calcutta, Jute Manufactures Development Council, 1998

ATIRA. *Workshop on Jute: The Golden Fibre.* Ahmedabad, Ahmedabad Textile Industry's Research Association, 1993